FOR ORGANS, PIANOS & ELECTRONIC KEYBOARDS

E-Z PLAY TODAY

153

50 GREAT SONGS

T0039750

To access audio visit:
www.halleonard.com/mylibrary

Enter Code
5932-9501-5312-1662

Audio arrangements by Larry Moore

ISBN 978-1-4950-0883-2

HAL•LEONARD® CORPORATION

7777 W. BLUEMOUND RD. P.O. BOX 13819 MILWAUKEE, WI 53213

Visit Hal Leonard Online at
www.halleonard.com

All I Ask of You
from THE PHANTOM OF THE OPERA

Registration 3
Rhythm: Ballad

Music by Andrew Lloyd Webber
Lyrics by Charles Hart
Additional Lyrics by Richard Stilgoe

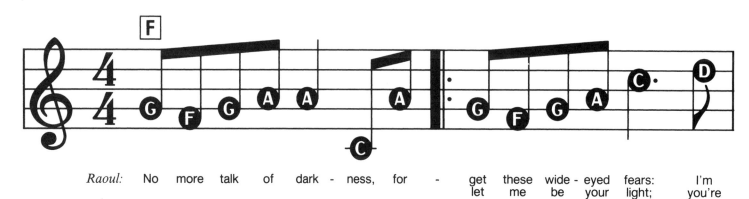

Raoul: No more talk of dark - ness, for - get these wide - eyed fears: I'm
let me be your light; I'm you're

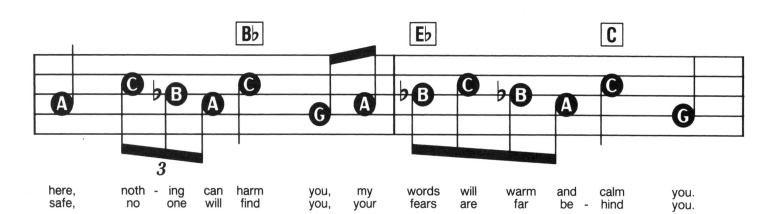

here, noth - ing can harm you, my words will warm and calm you.
safe, no one will find you, my your fears are far be - hind you.

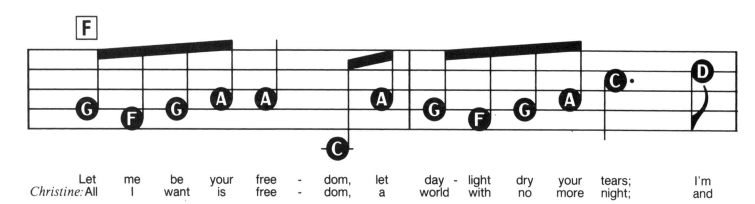

Let me be your free - dom, let day - light dry your tears; I'm
Christine: All I want is free - dom, a world with no more night; and

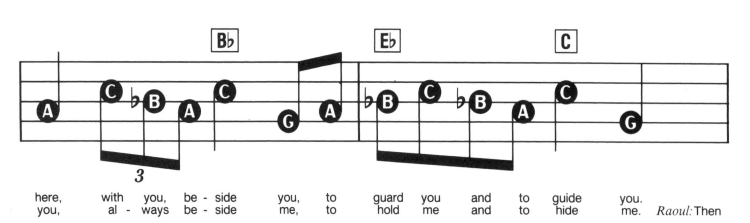

here, with you, be - side you, to guard you and to guide you.
you, al - ways be - side me, to hold me and to hide me. *Raoul:* Then

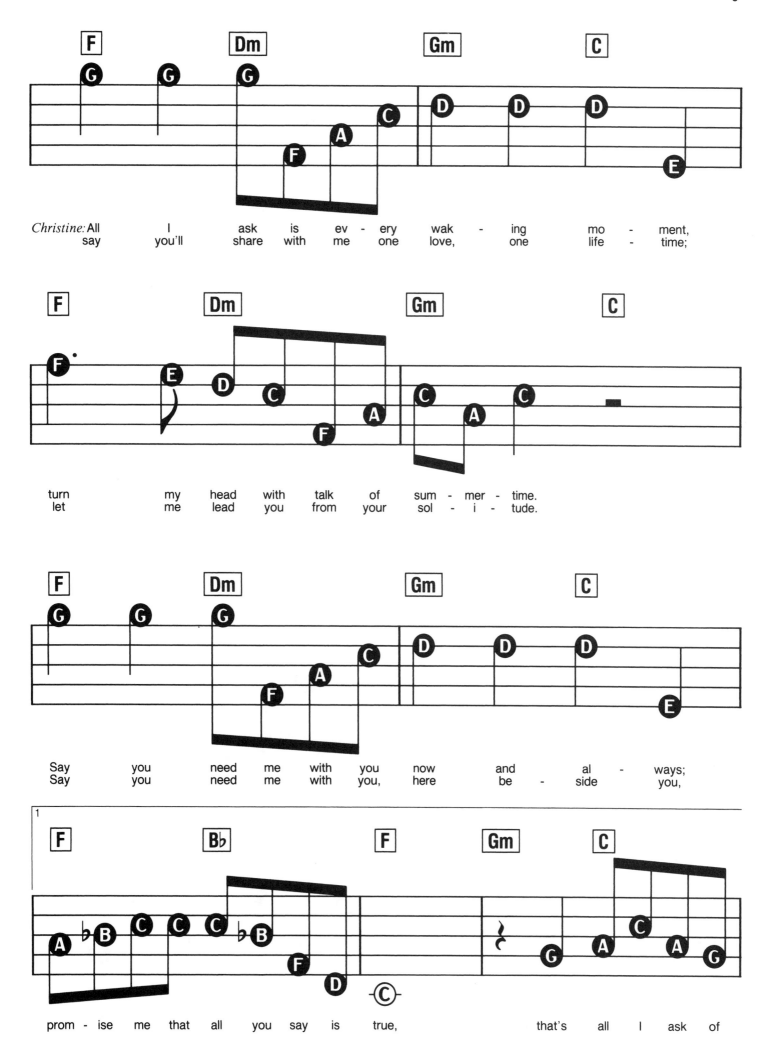

5

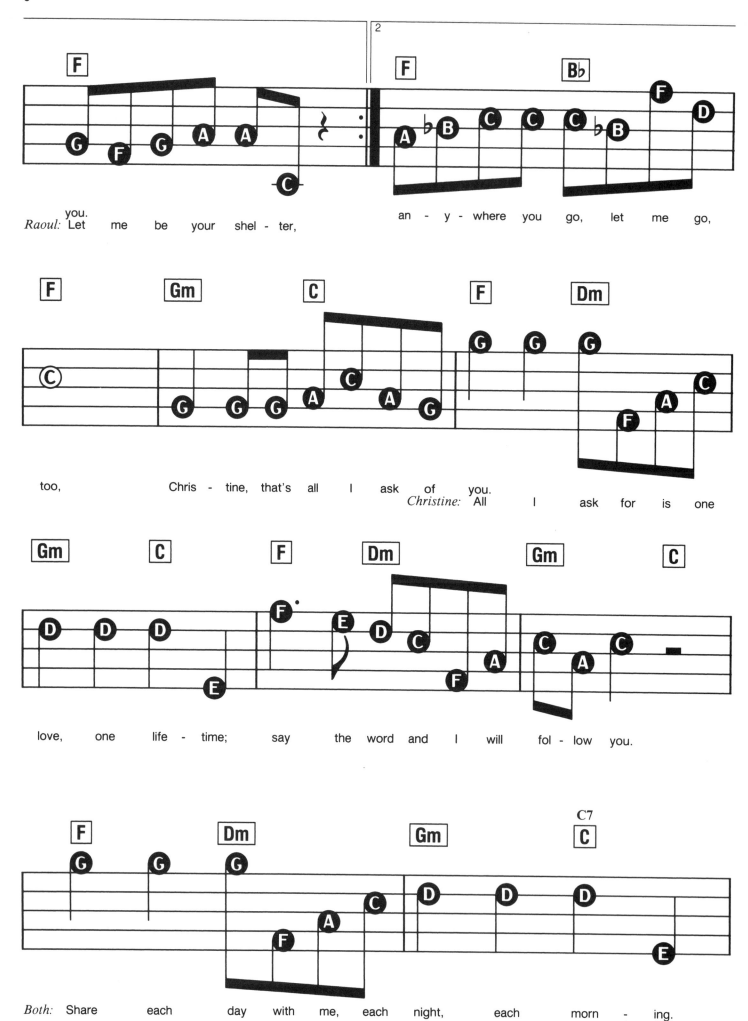

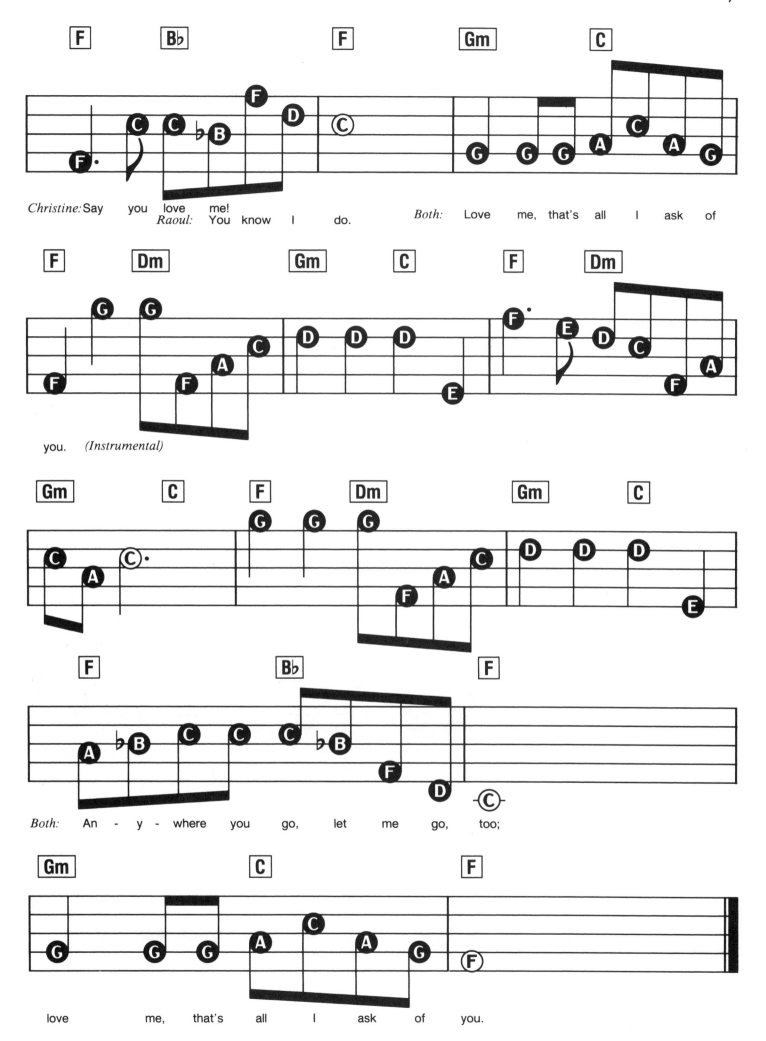

Christine: Say you love me! Raoul: You know I do. Both: Love me, that's all I ask of

you. (Instrumental)

Both: An - y - where you go, let me go, too;

love me, that's all I ask of you.

All the Things You Are

from VERY WARM FOR MAY

Registration 2
Rhythm: Ballad or Swing

Lyrics by Oscar Hammerstein II
Music by Jerome Kern

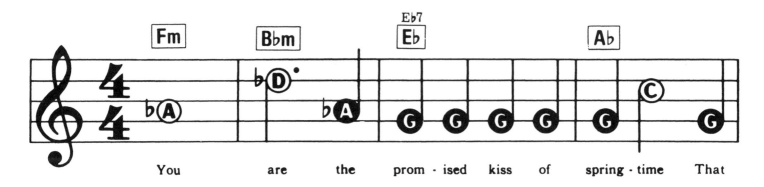

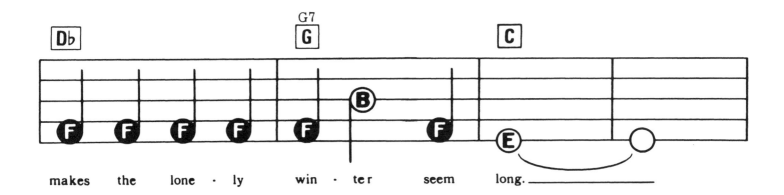

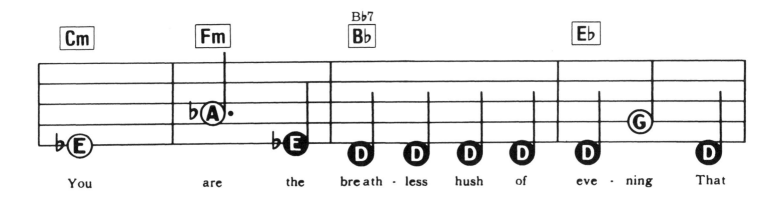

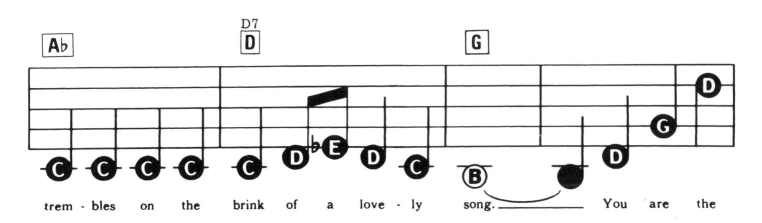

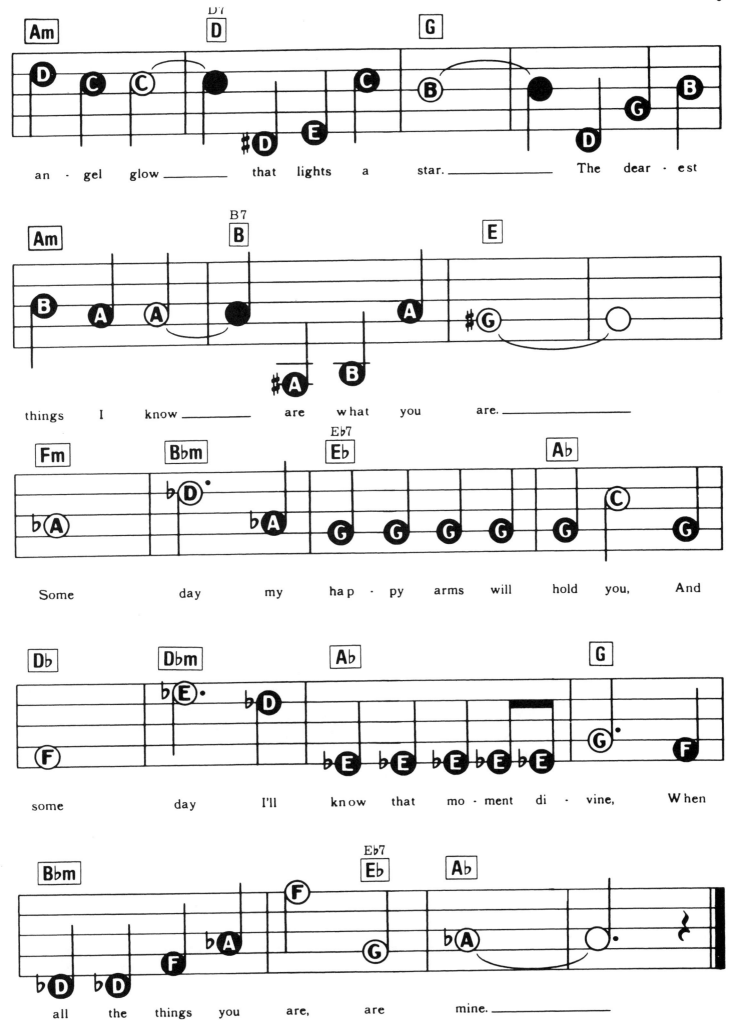

And So It Goes

Registration 10
Rhythm: Waltz or None

Words and Music by
Billy Joel

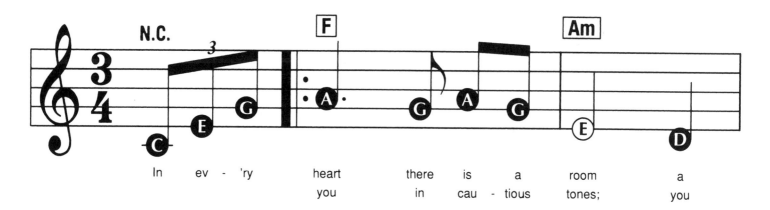

In ev - 'ry heart there is a room a
you in cau - tious tones; you

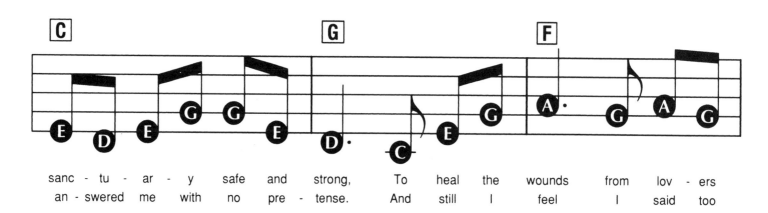

sanc - tu - ar - y safe and strong, To heal the wounds from lov - ers
an - swered me with no pre - tense. And still I feel I said too

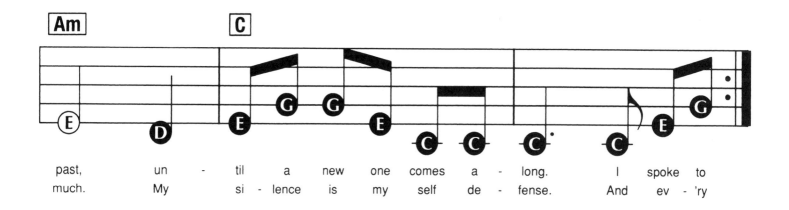

past, un - til a new one comes a - long. I spoke to
much. My si - lence is my self de - fense. And ev - 'ry

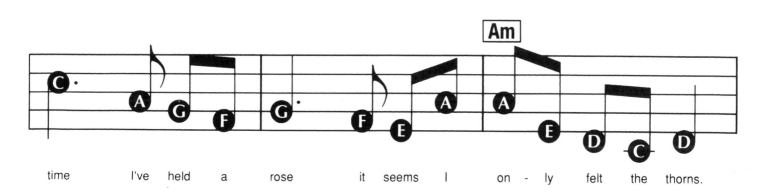

time I've held a rose it seems I on - ly felt the thorns.

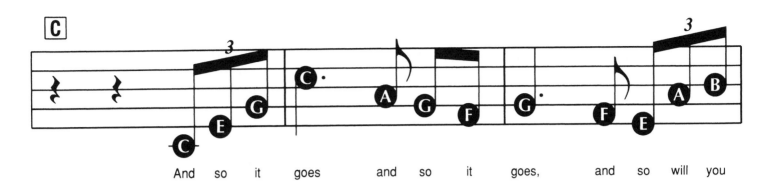

And so it goes and so it goes, and so will you

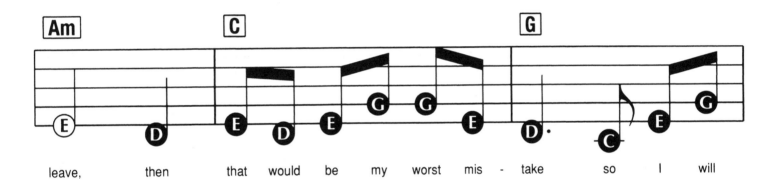

soon I sup - pose. _____ But if my si - lence made you

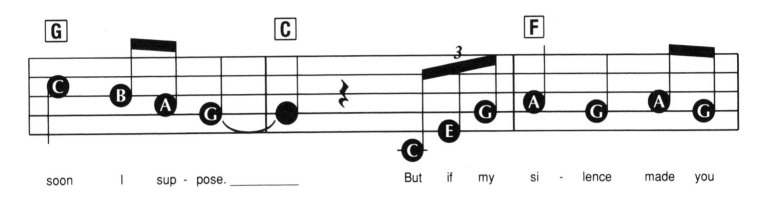

leave, then that would be my worst mis - take so I will

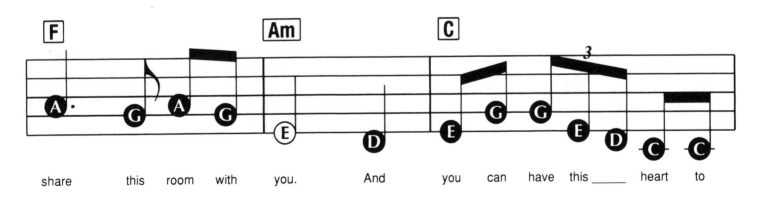

share this room with you. And you can have this ____ heart to

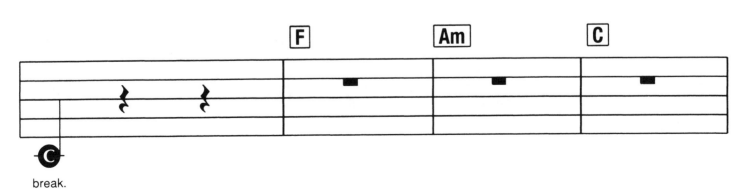

break.

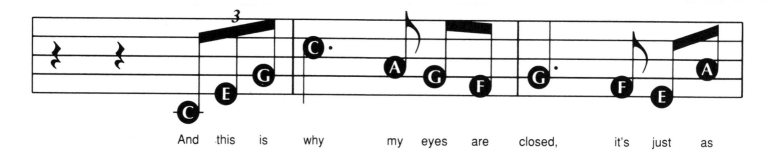

And this is why my eyes are closed, it's just as

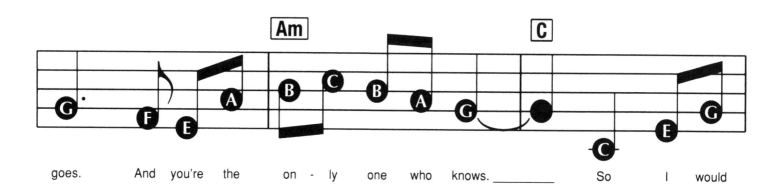

well for all I've seen. And so it goes and so it

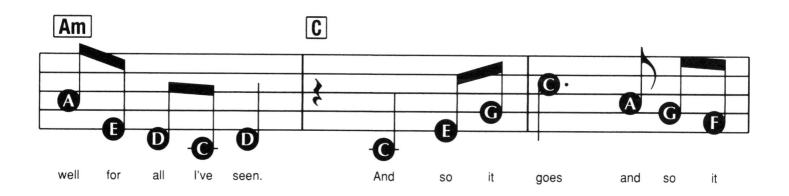

goes. And you're the on - ly one who knows. _____ So I would

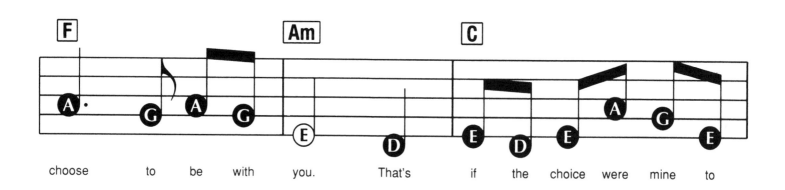

choose to be with you. That's if the choice were mine to

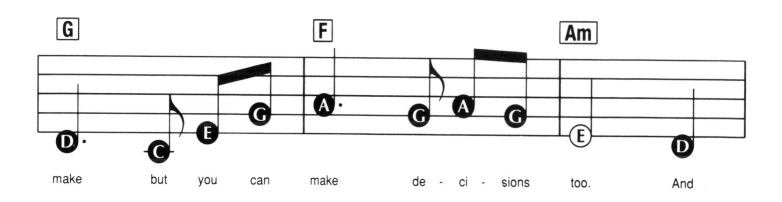

make but you can make de - ci - sions too. And

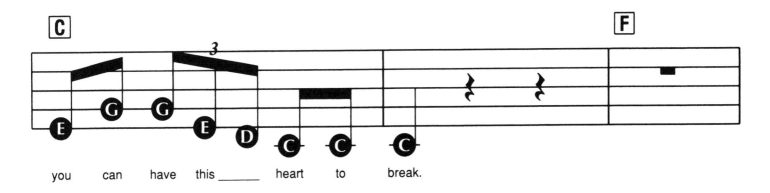

you can have this _____ heart to break.

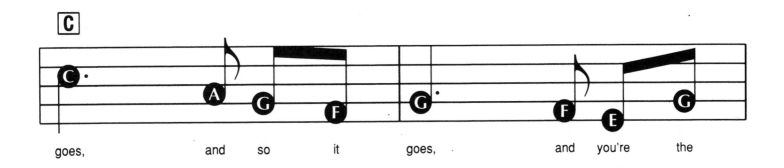

And so it

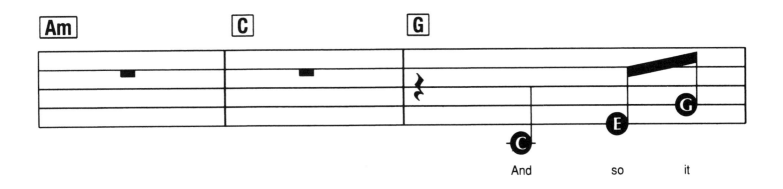

goes, and so it goes, and you're the

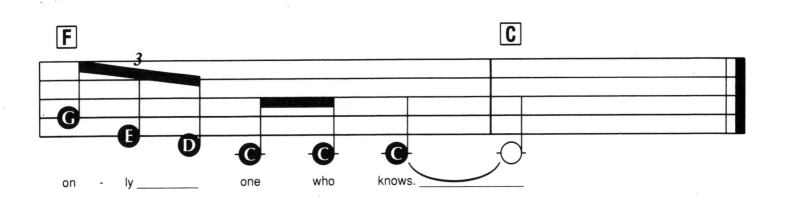

on - ly _____ one who knows. _____

At Last
from ORCHESTRA WIVES

Registration 3
Rhythm: Ballad or Swing

Lyric by Mack Gordon
Music by Harry Warren

At
last _____ my love has come a-
last _____ the skies a - bove are

long, _____ my lone - ly days are o - ver _____
blue, _____ my heart was wrapped in clo - ver _____

_____ and life is like a song. _____ At
_____ the night I looked at

you. I found a dream that I can

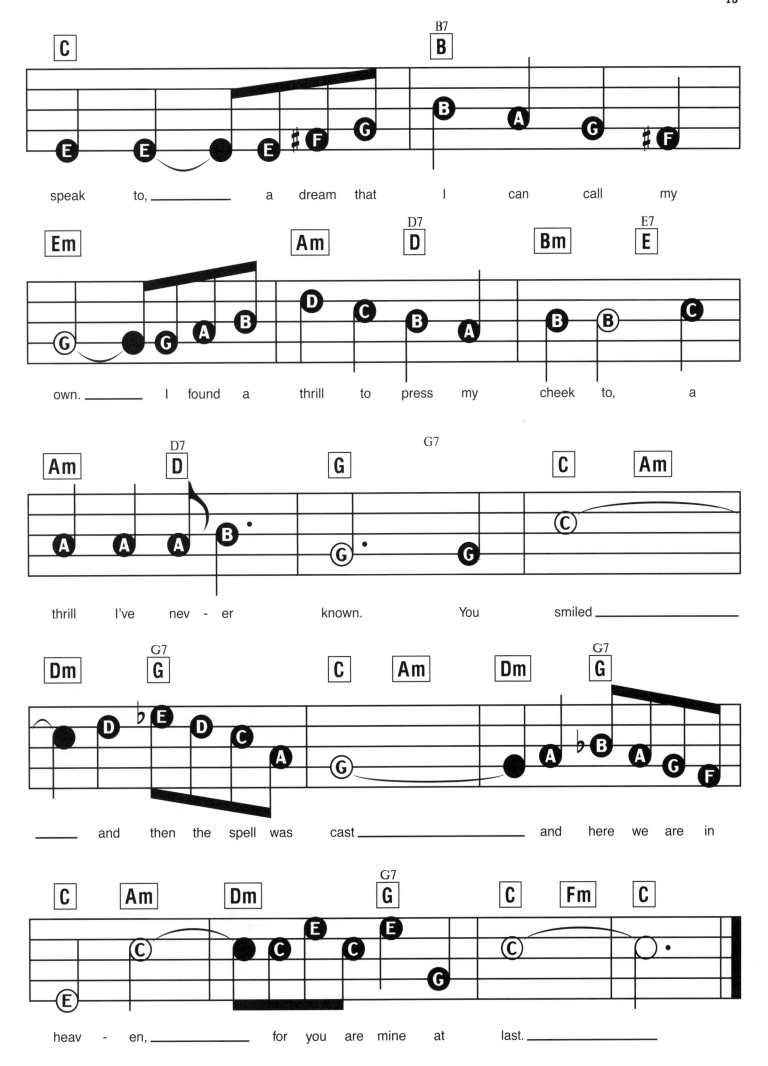

Autumn Leaves

Registration 2
Rhythm: Fox Trot or Ballad

English lyric by Johnny Mercer
French lyric by Jacques Prevert
Music by Joseph Kosma

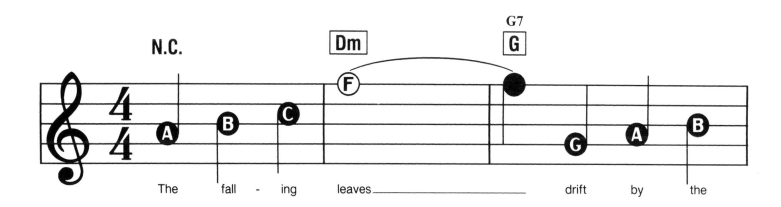

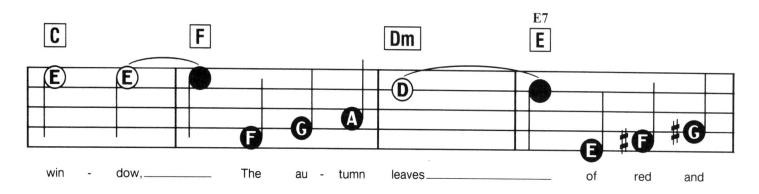

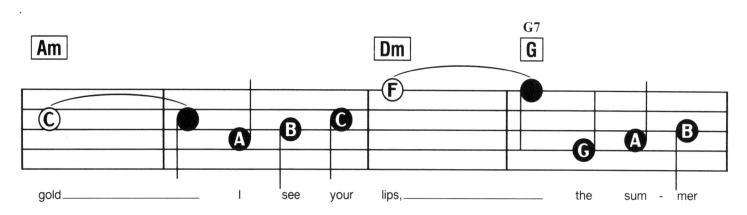

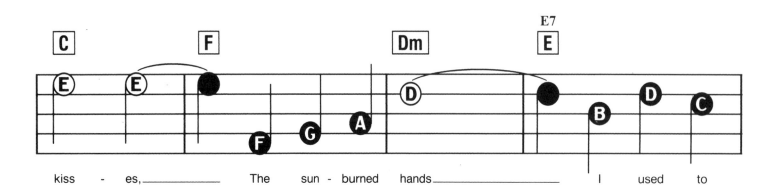

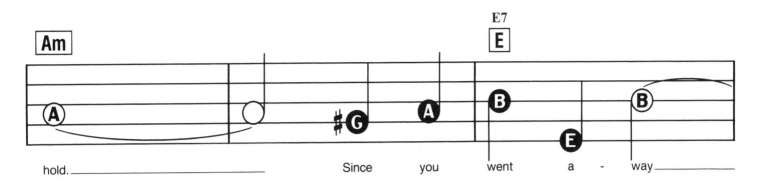

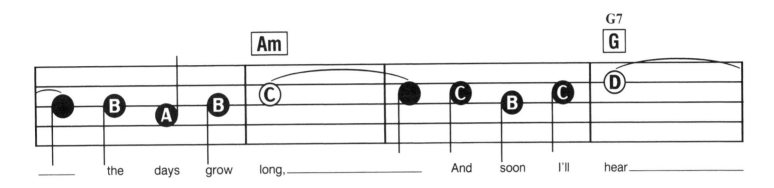

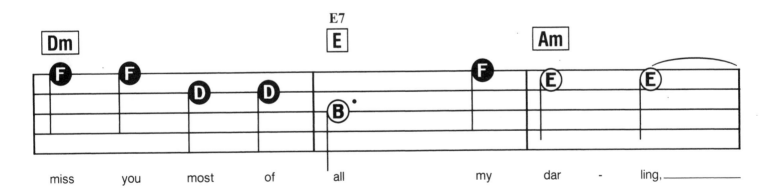

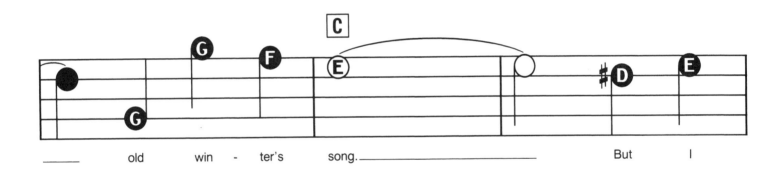

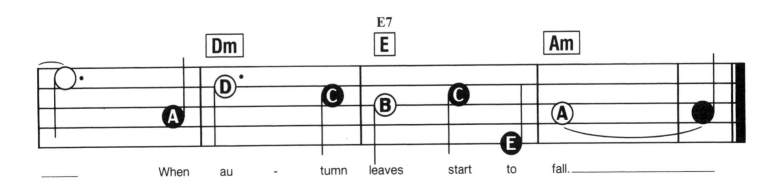

Beer Barrel Polka
(Roll Out the Barrel)
based on the European success "Skoda Laasky"

Registration 5
Rhythm: Polka or March

By Lew Brown, Wladimir A. Timm,
Jaromir Vejvoda and Vasek Zeman

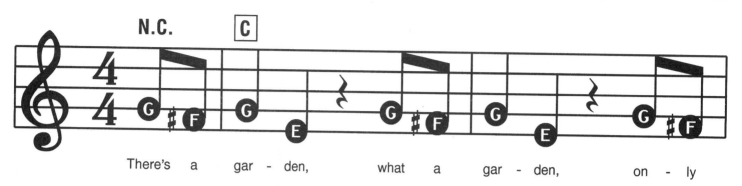

There's a gar - den, what a gar - den, on - ly

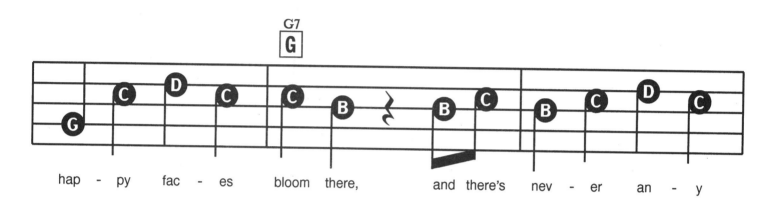

hap - py fac - es bloom there, and there's nev - er an - y

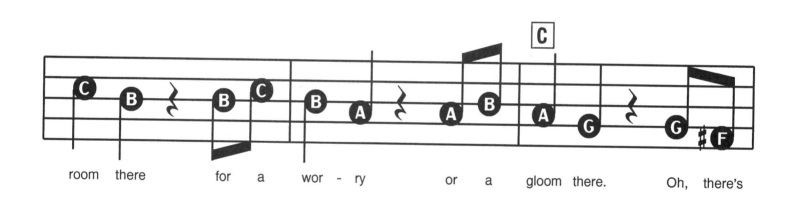

room there for a wor - ry or a gloom there. Oh, there's

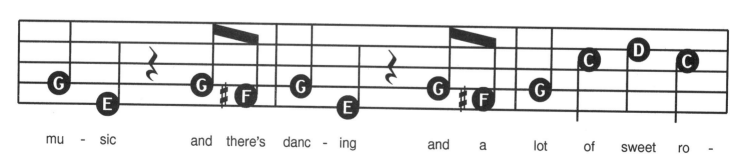

mu - sic and there's danc - ing and a lot of sweet ro -

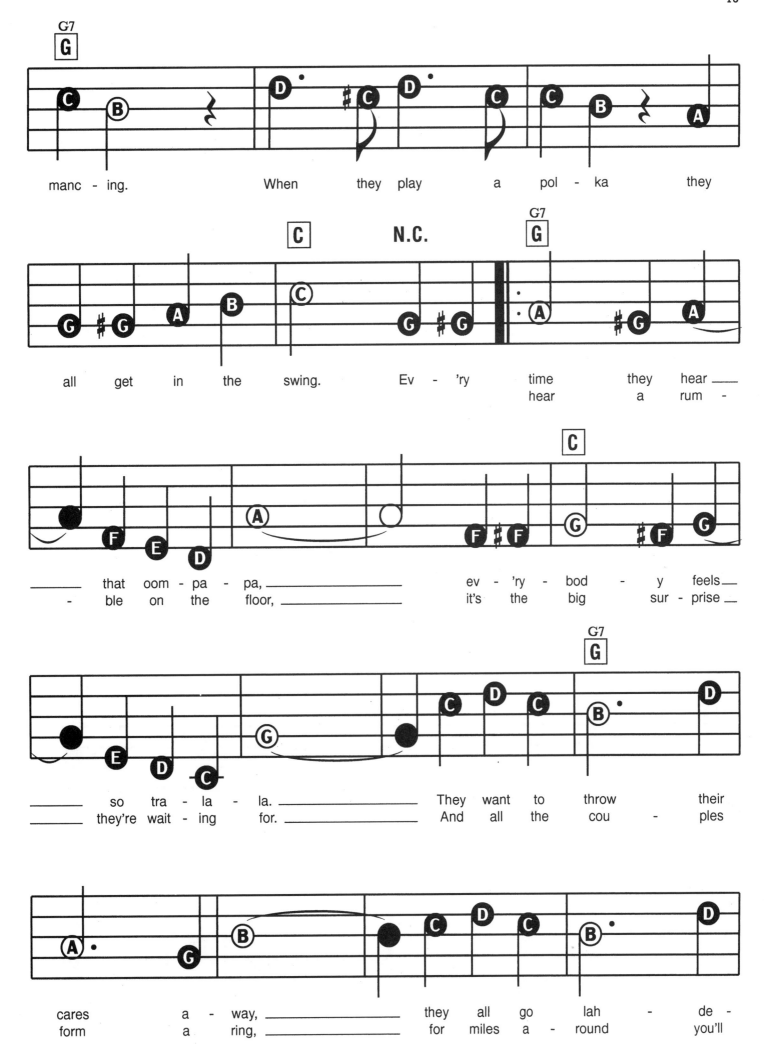

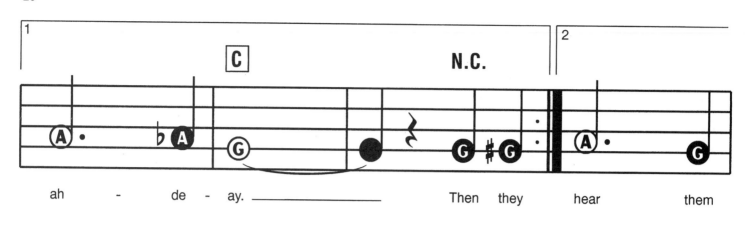

ah - de - ay. _____ Then they hear them

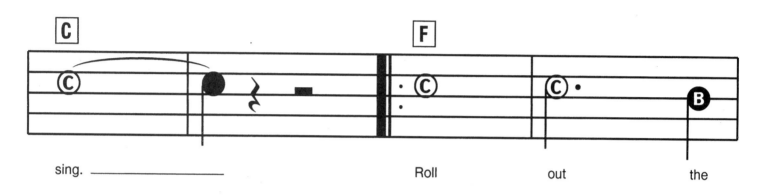

sing. _____ Roll out the

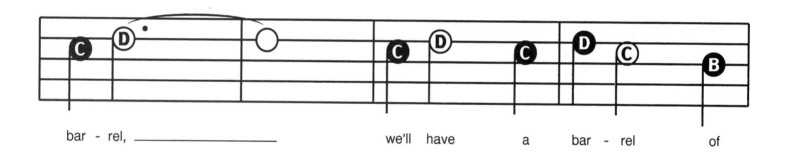

bar - rel, _____ we'll have a bar - rel of

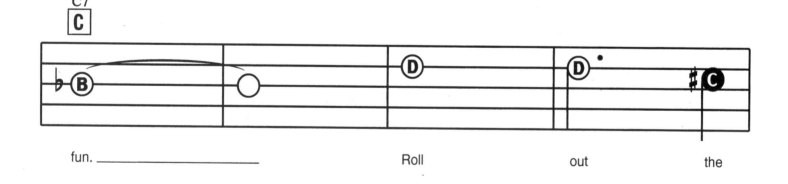

fun. _____ Roll out the

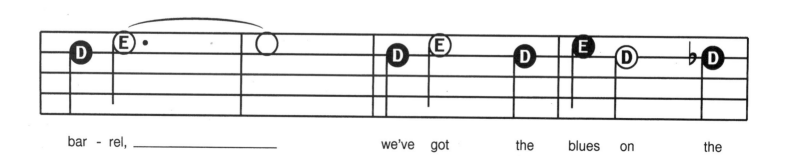

bar - rel, _____ we've got the blues on the

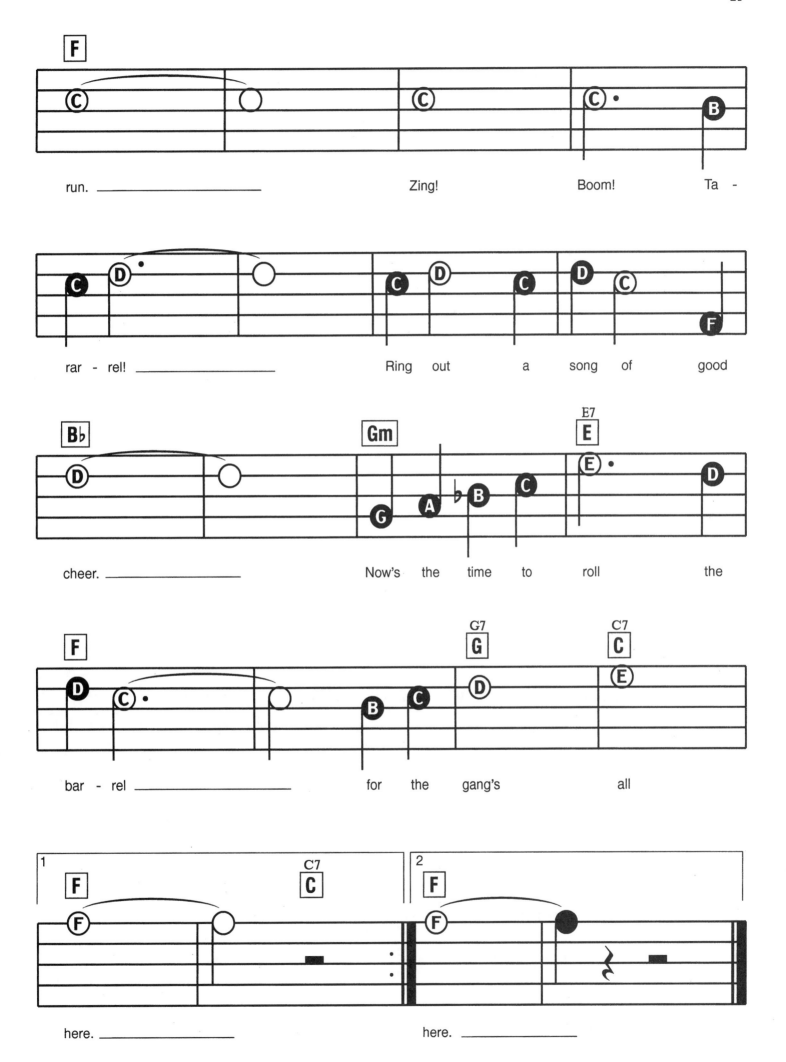

Bein' Green

Registration 3
Rhythm: Ballad

Words and Music by
Joe Raposo

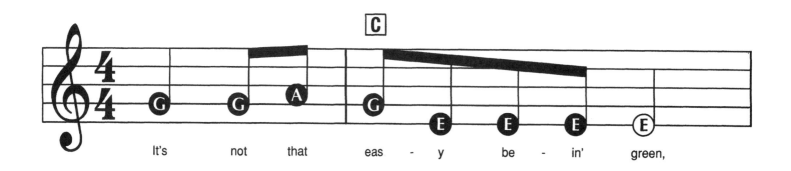

It's not that eas - y be - in' green,

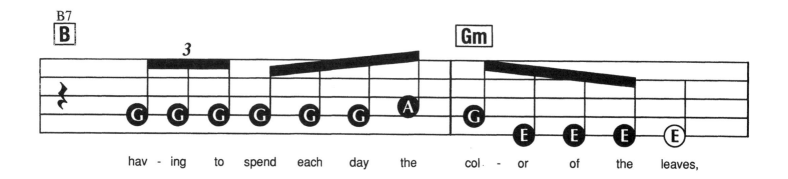

hav - ing to spend each day the col - or of the leaves,

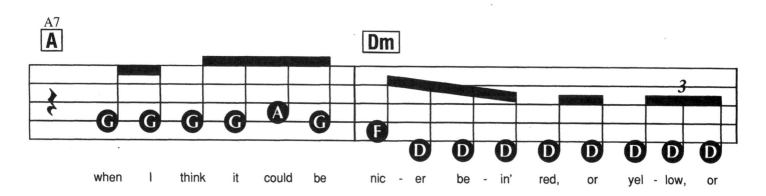

when I think it could be nic - er be - in' red, or yel - low, or

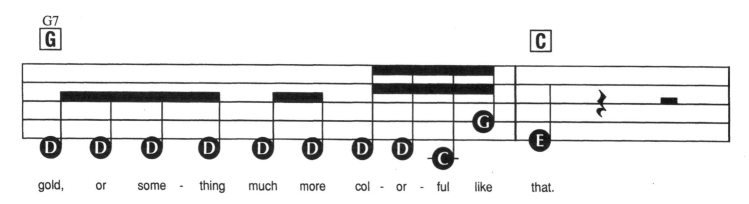

gold, or some - thing much more col - or - ful like that.

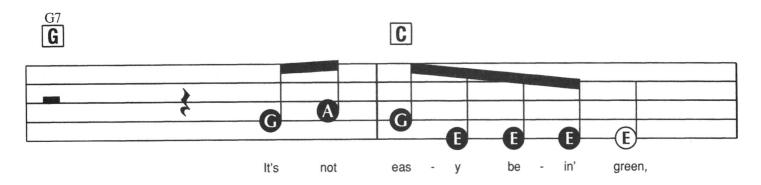

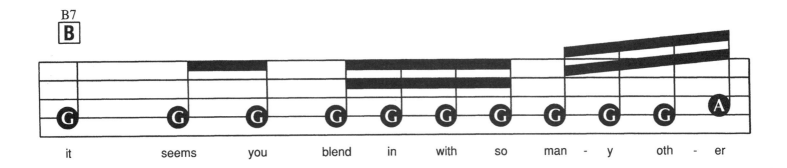

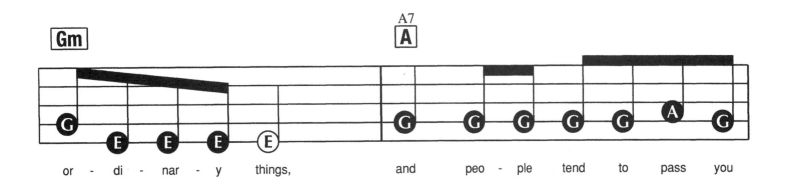

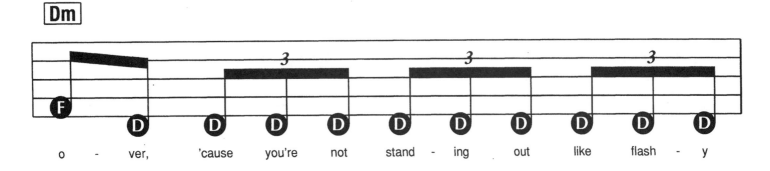

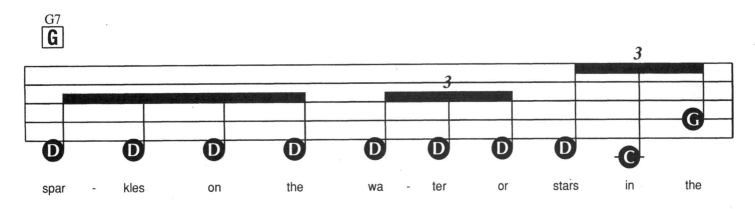

24

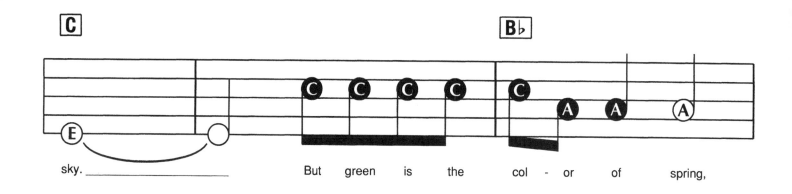

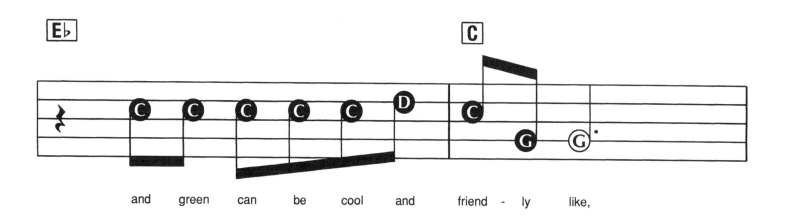

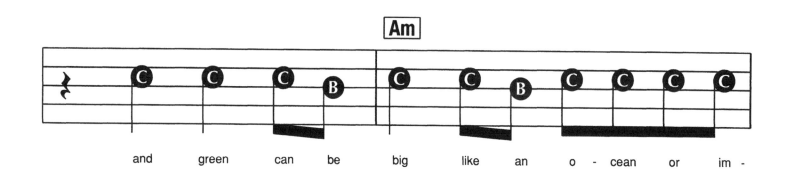

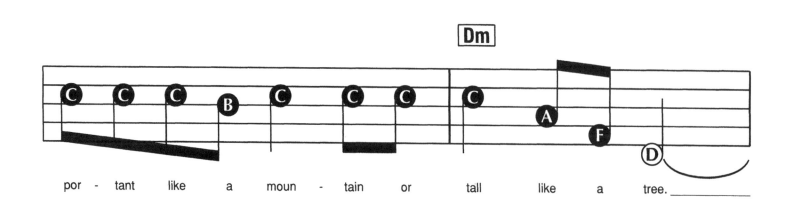

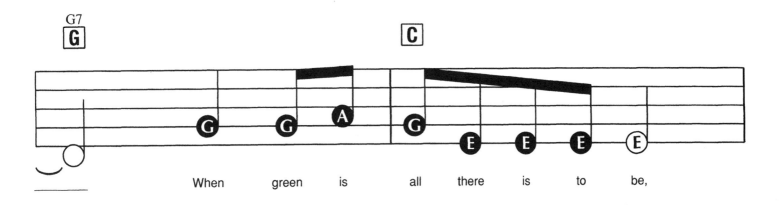

When green is all there is to be,

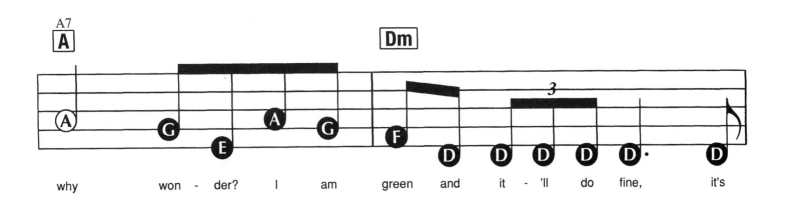

it could make you won - der why, but why won - der,

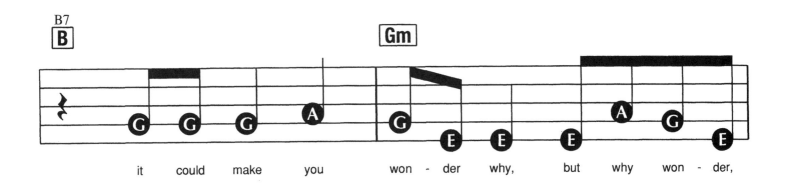

why won - der? I am green and it - 'll do fine, it's

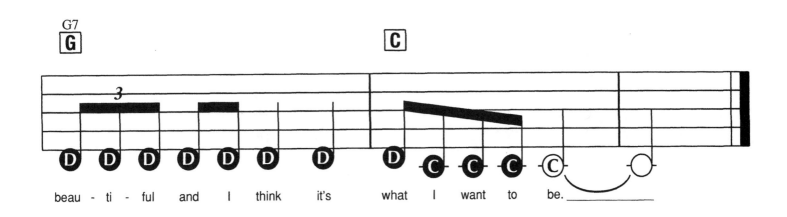

beau - ti - ful and I think it's what I want to be. _____

Blackbird

Registration 8
Rhythm: Rock

Words and Music by John Lennon
and Paul McCartney

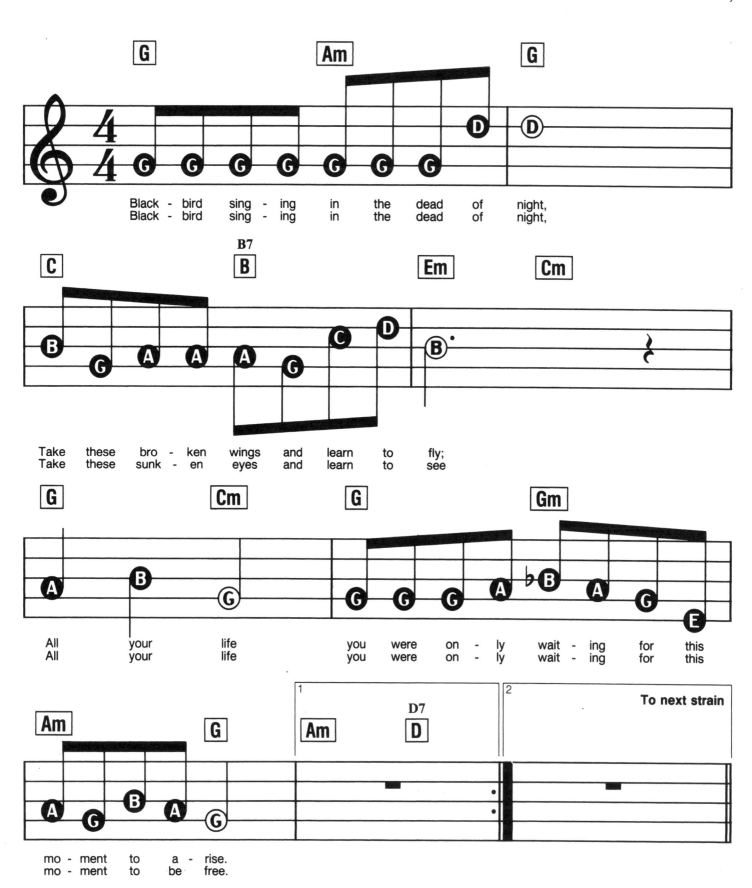

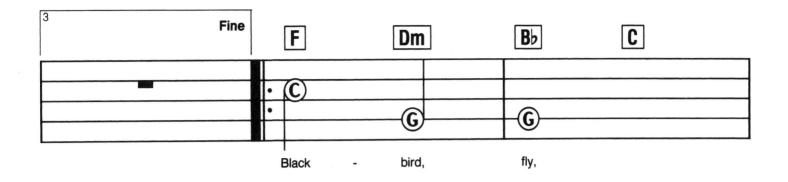

Black - bird, fly,

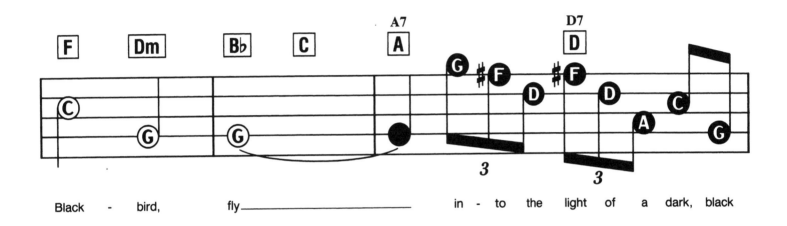

Black - bird, fly_____ in - to the light of a dark, black

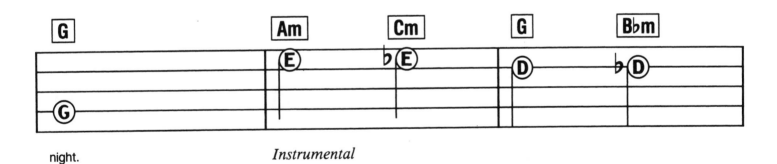

night.   *Instrumental*

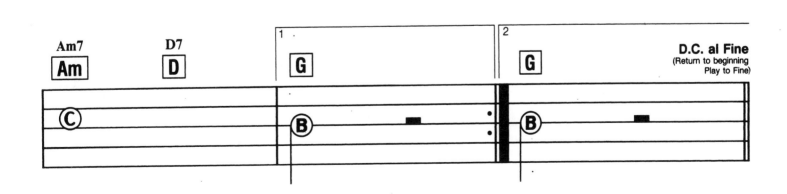

D.C. al Fine
(Return to beginning
Play to Fine)

Blowin' in the Wind

Registration 4
Rhythm: Ballad or Fox Trot

Words and Music by
Bob Dylan

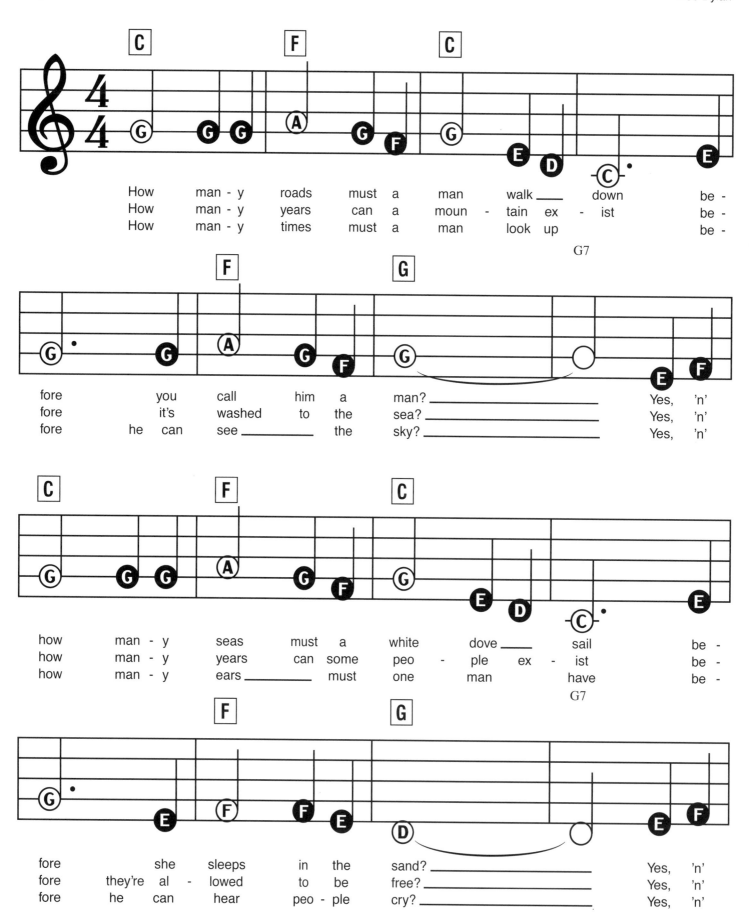

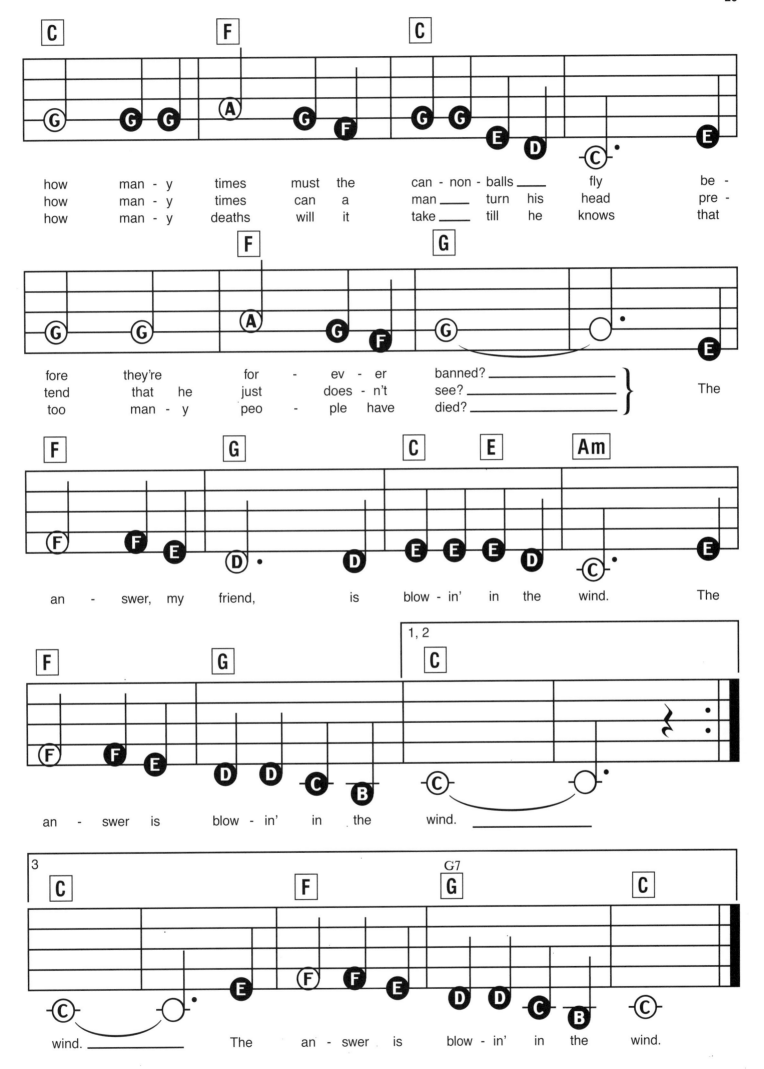

Boot Scootin' Boogie

Registration 2
Rhythm: Swing or Country Shuffle

Words and Music by
Ronnie Dunn

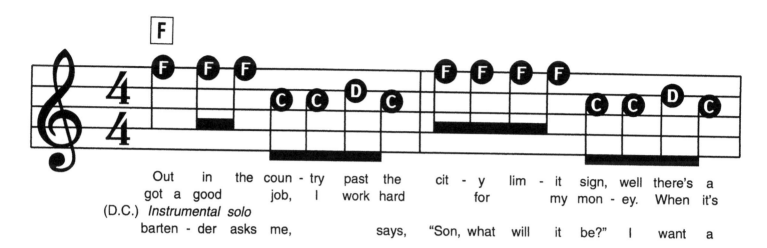

Out in the coun - try past the cit - y lim - it sign, well there's a
got a good job, I work hard for my mon - ey. When it's
(D.C.) *Instrumental solo*
barten - der asks me, says, "Son, what will it be?" I want a

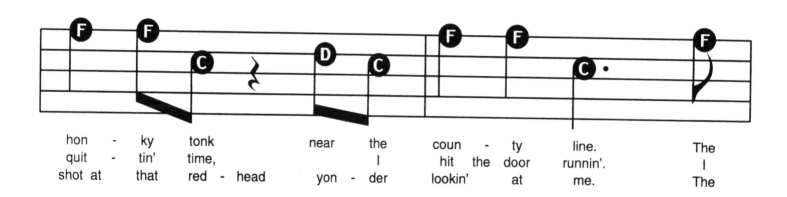

hon - ky tonk near the coun - ty line. The
quit - tin' time, I hit the door runnin'. The I
shot at that red - head yon - der lookin' at me. The

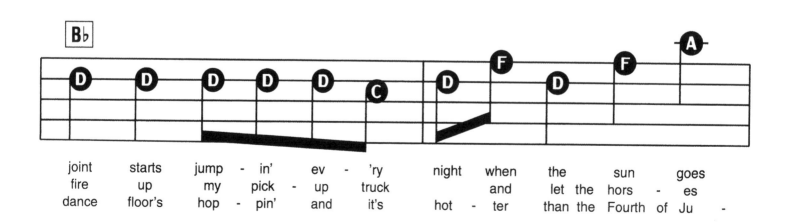

joint starts jump - in' ev - 'ry night when the sun goes
fire up my pick - up truck and let the hors - es
dance floor's hop - pin' and it's hot - ter than the Fourth of Ju -

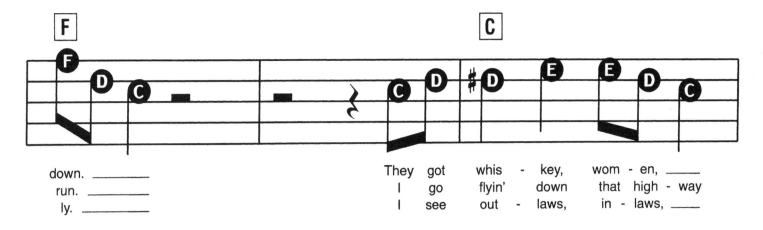

down. _____
run. _____
ly. _____

They got whis - key, wom - en, _____
I go flyin' down that high - way
I see out - laws, in - laws, _____

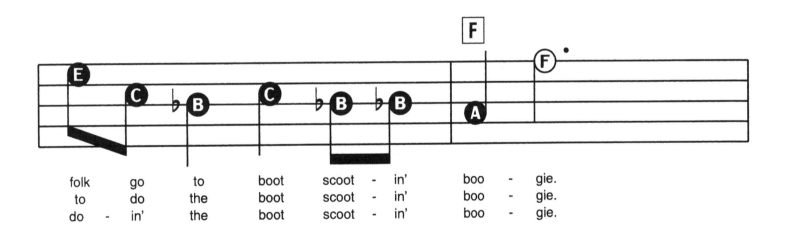

mu - sic and smoke. _____
to that hide - a - way _____
crooks and straights _____

It's where all the cow - boy
stuck out in the woods,
all out mak - in' it shake

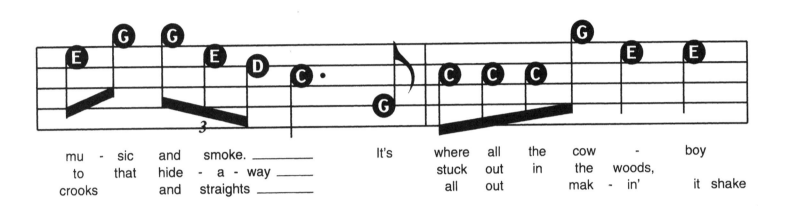

folk go to the boot scoot - in' boo - gie.
to do the boot scoot - in' boo - gie.
do - in' the boot scoot - in' boo - gie.

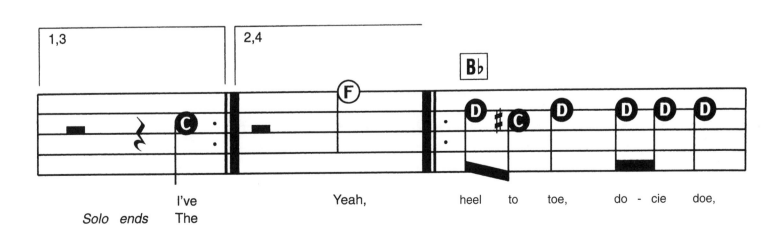

1,3

2,4

B♭

I've
Solo ends The

Yeah, heel to toe, do - cie doe,

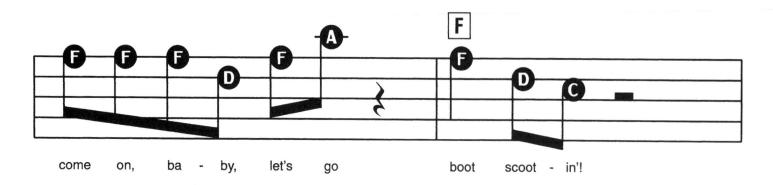

come on, ba - by, let's go   boot scoot - in'!

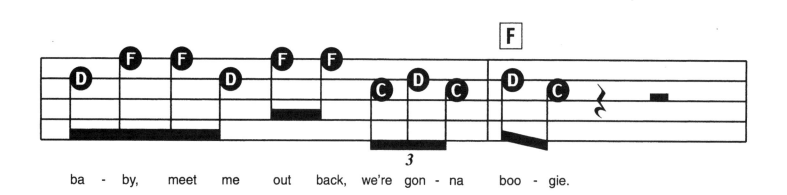

Whoa,   Cad - il - lac,   Black - jack,

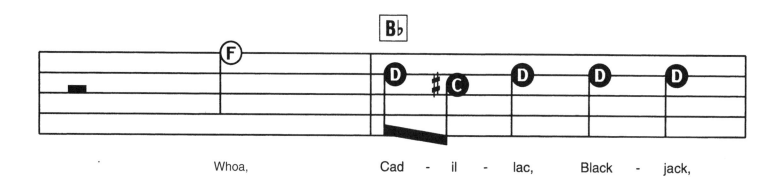

ba - by, meet me out back, we're gon - na boo - gie.

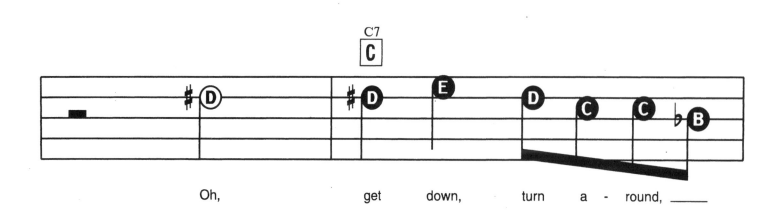

Oh,   get down, turn a - round, _____

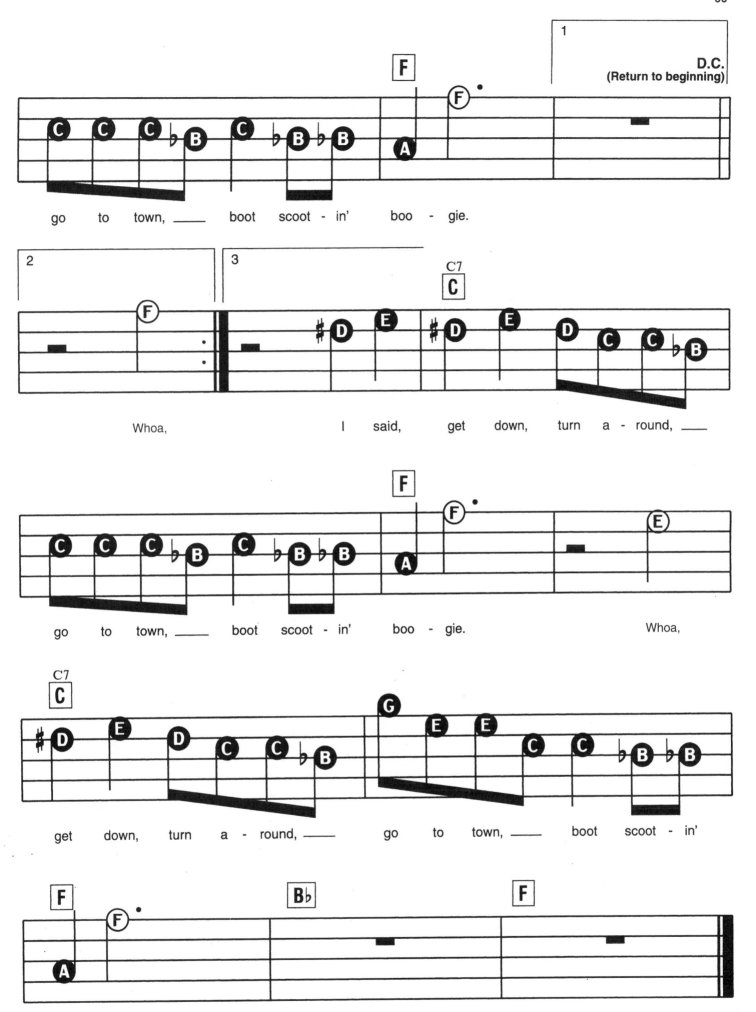

Both Sides Now

Registration 4
Rhythm: Pops or 8-Beat

Words and Music by
Joni Mitchell

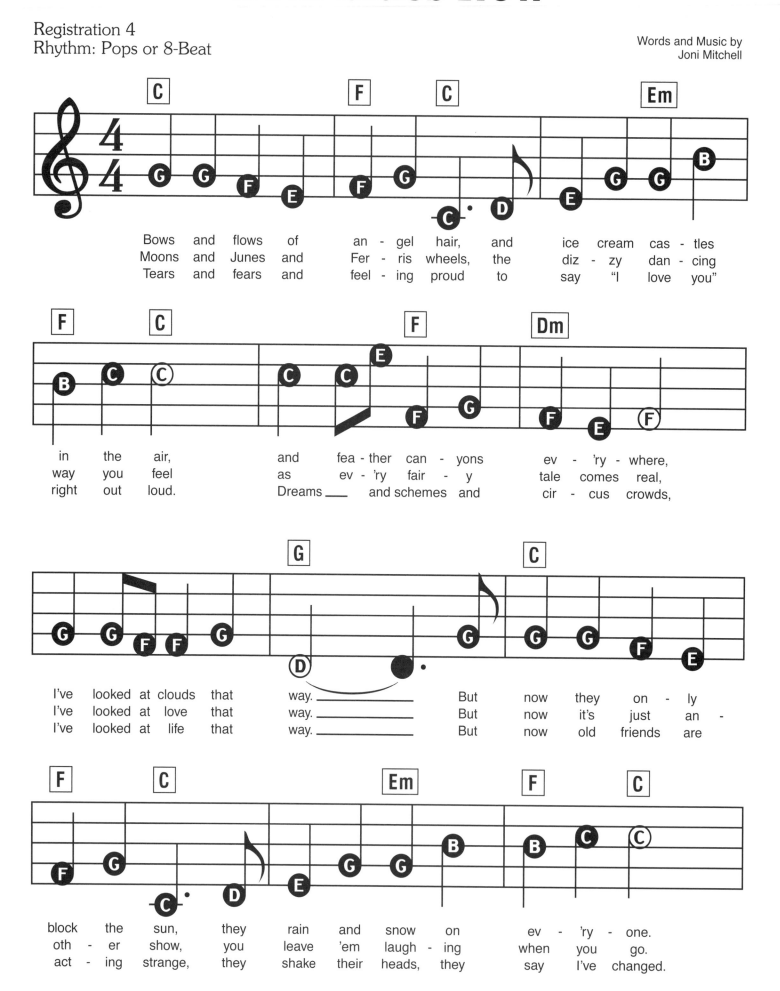

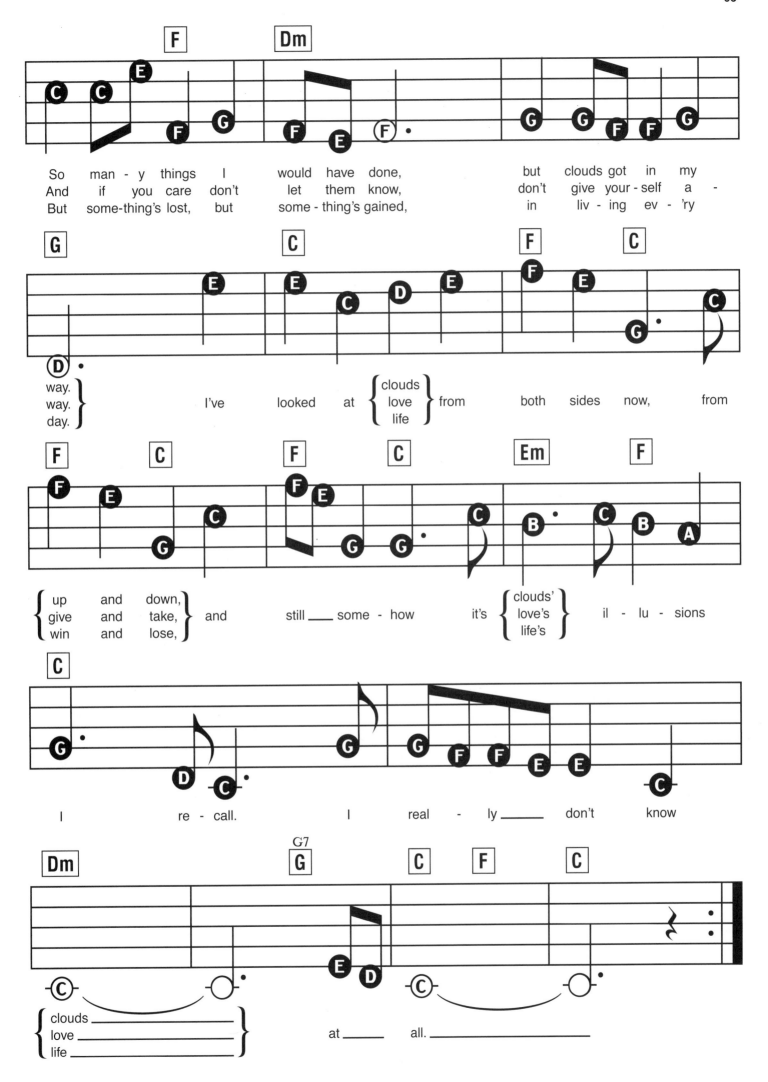

Bridge Over Troubled Water

Registration 3
Rhythm: Slow Rock or Ballad

Words and Music by
Paul Simon

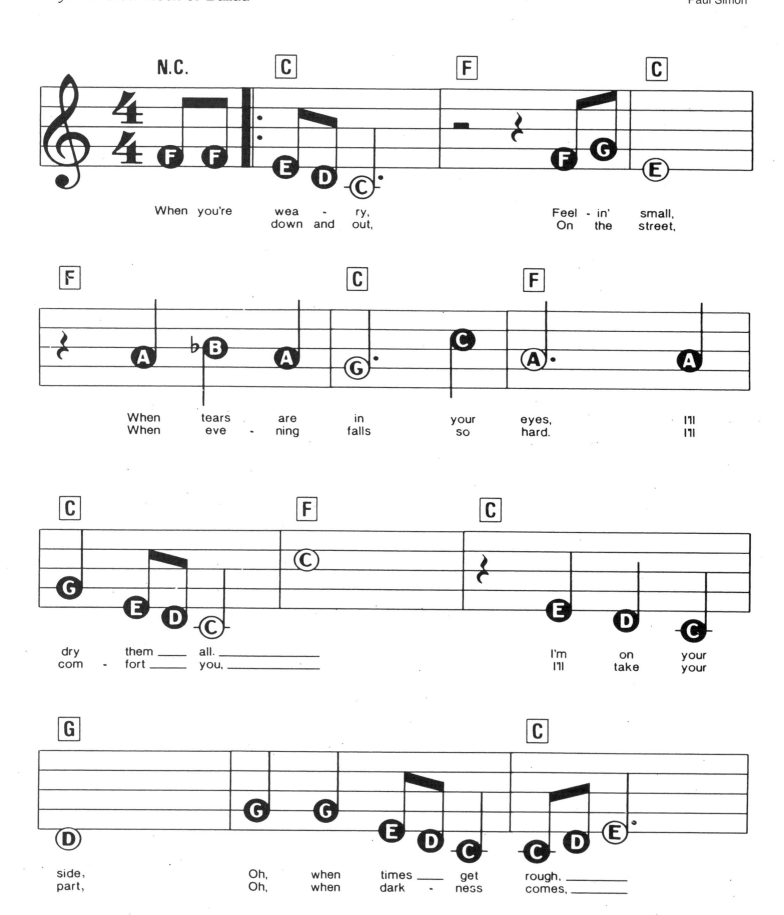

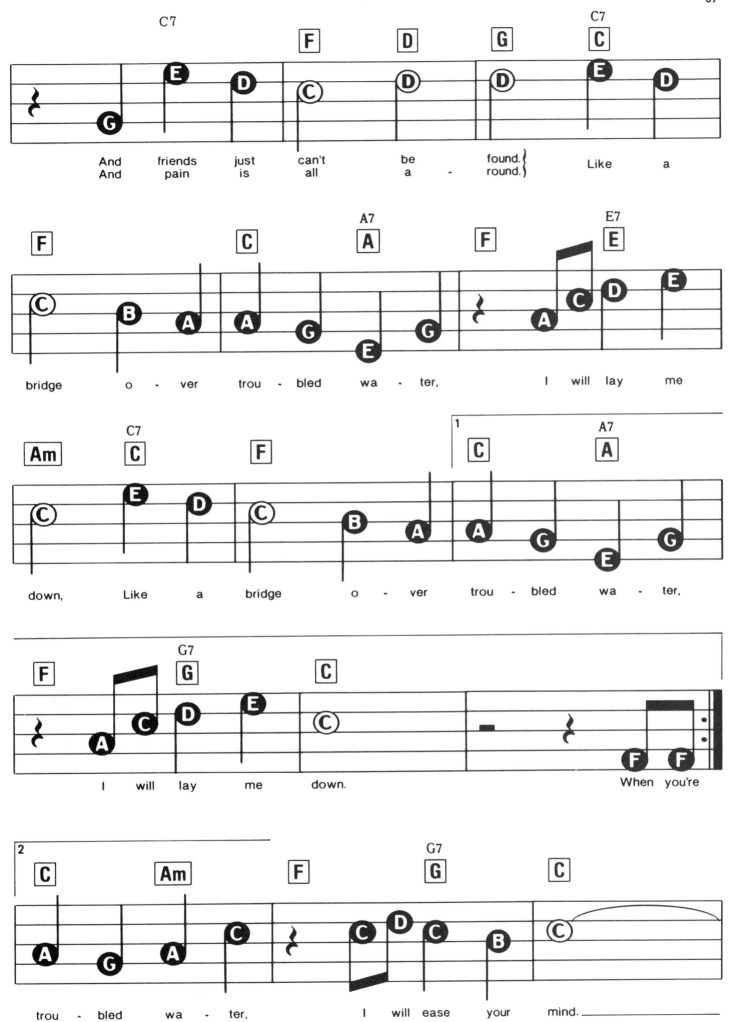

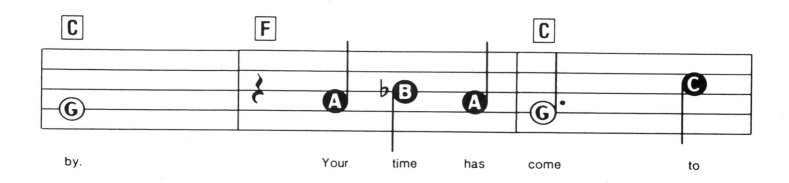

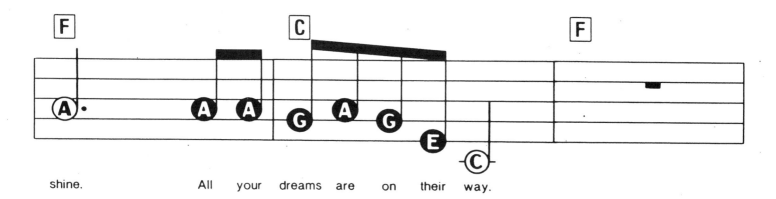

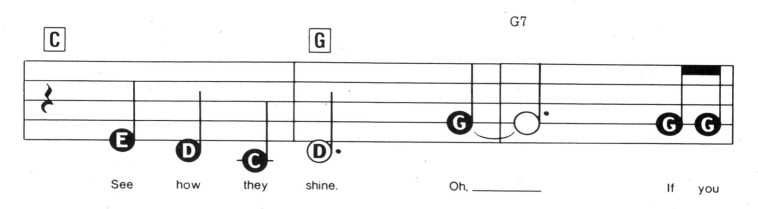

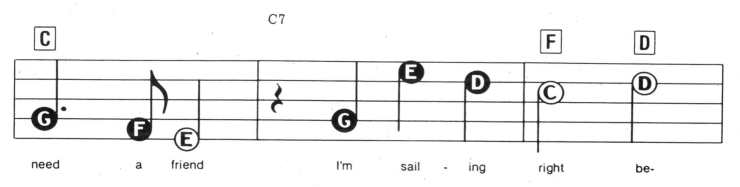

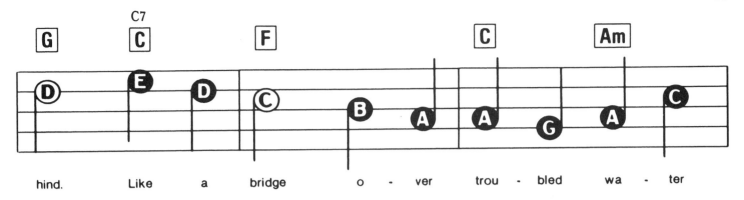

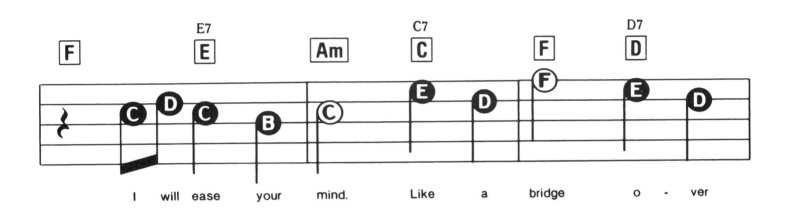

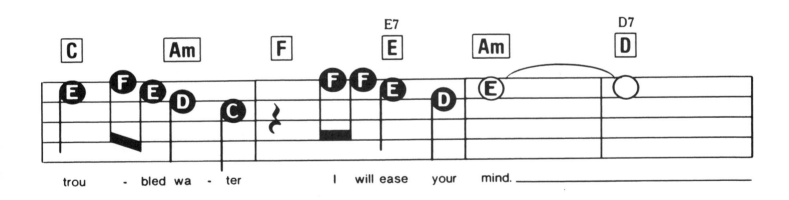

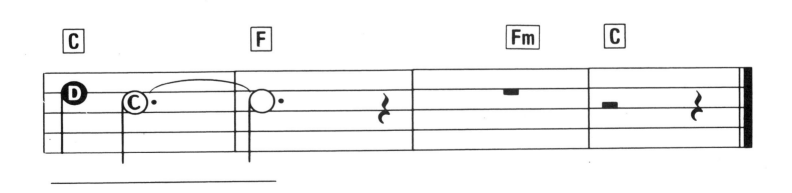

Charade
from CHARADE

Registration 3
Rhythm: Waltz

Music by Henry Mancini
Words by Johnny Mercer

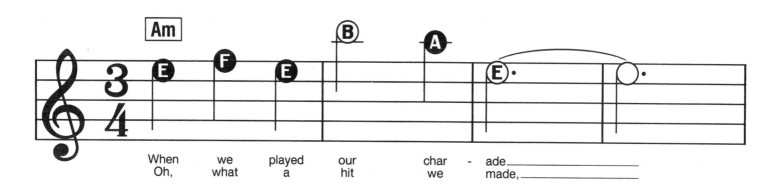

When we played our char - ade_____
Oh, what a we hit made,_____

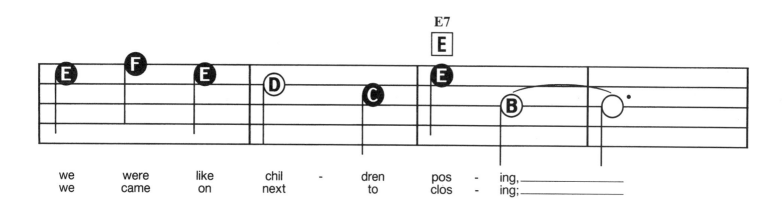

we were like chil - dren pos - ing,_____
we came on next to clos - ing;_____

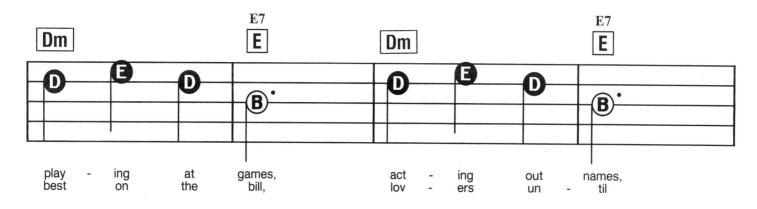

play - ing at games, act - ing out names,
best on the bill, lov - ers un - til

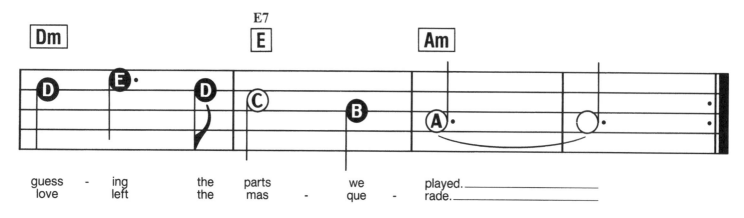

guess - ing the parts we played._____
love left the mas - que - rade._____

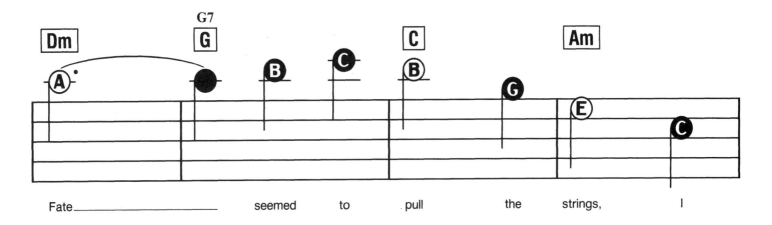

Fate seemed to pull the strings, I

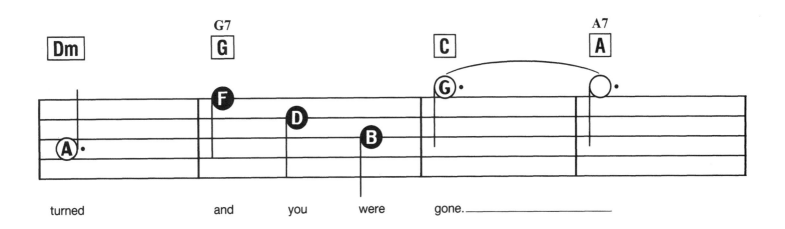

turned and you were gone.

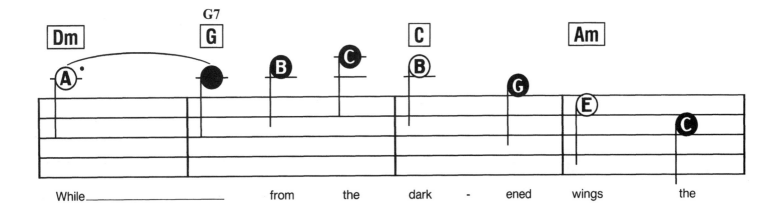

While from the dark - ened wings the

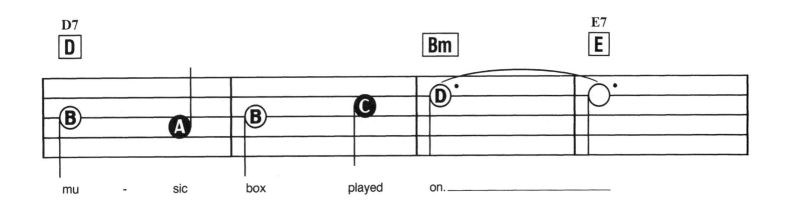

mu - sic box played on.

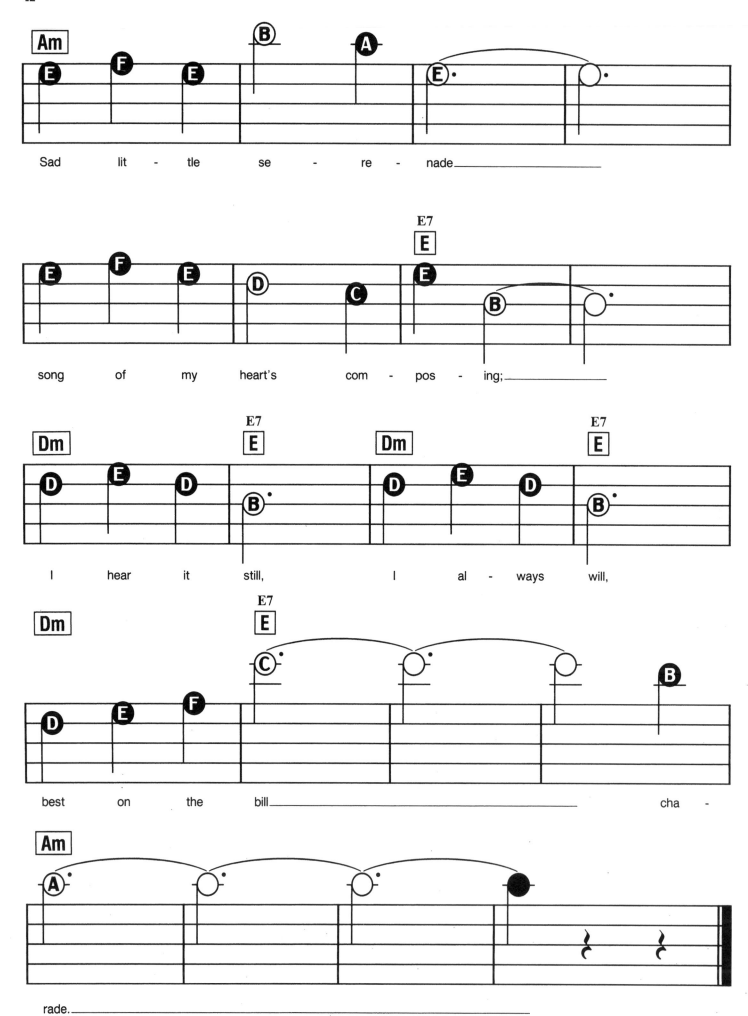

Chattanooga Choo Choo

Registration 9
Rhythm: Swing

Words by Mack Gordon
Music by Harry Warren

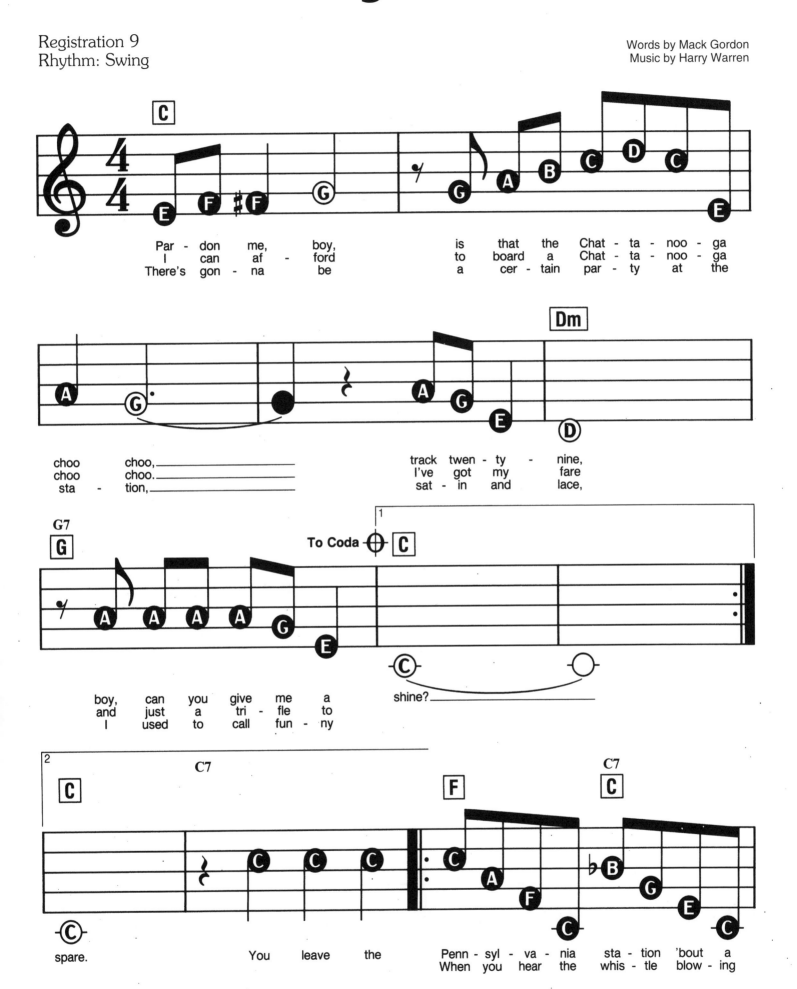

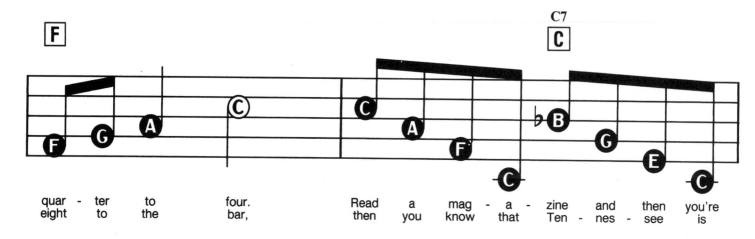

quar - ter to four.
eight to the bar,

Read a mag - a - zine and then you're
then you know that Ten - nes - see is

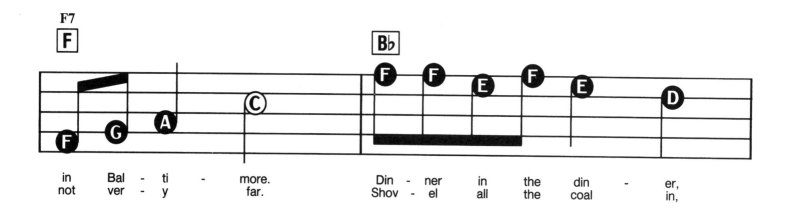

in Bal - ti - more.
not ver - y far.

Din - ner in the din - er,
Shov - el all the coal in,

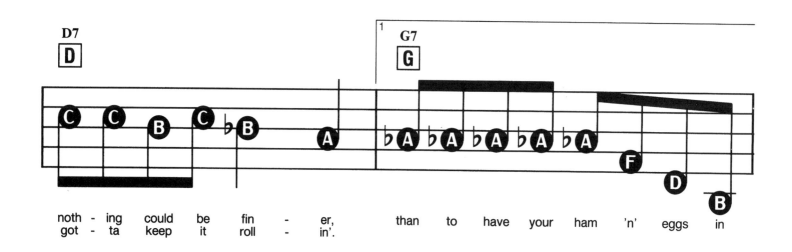

noth - ing could be fin - er,
got - ta keep it roll - in'.

than to have your ham 'n' eggs in

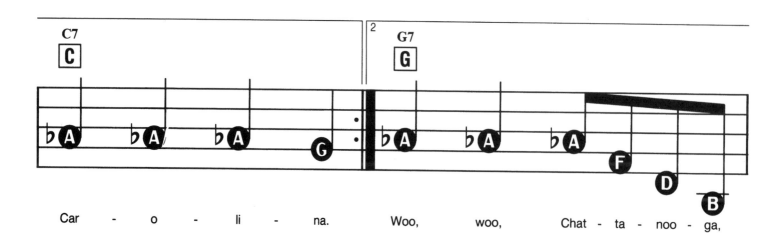

Car - o - li - na. Woo, woo, Chat - ta - noo - ga,

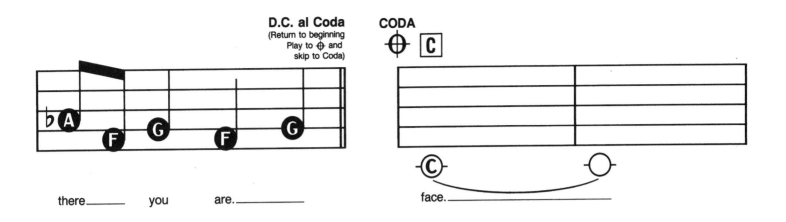

there_____ you   are._____

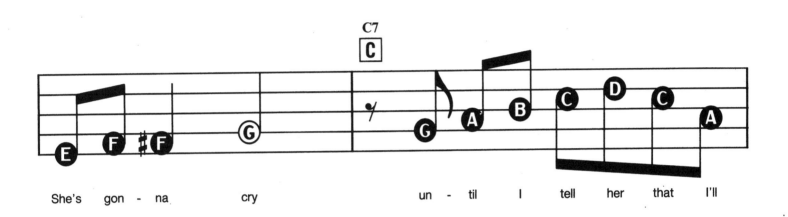

She's gon - na   cry   un - til   I   tell her that I'll

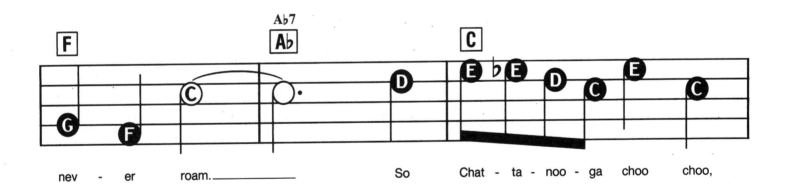

nev - er   roam._____   So   Chat - ta - noo - ga choo   choo,

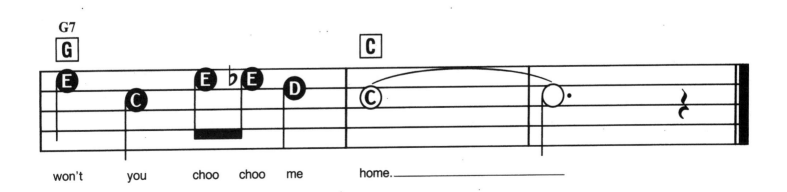

won't you   choo choo me   home._____

Cracklin' Rosie

Registration 5
Rhythm: Fox Trot or Ballad

Words and Music by
Neil Diamond

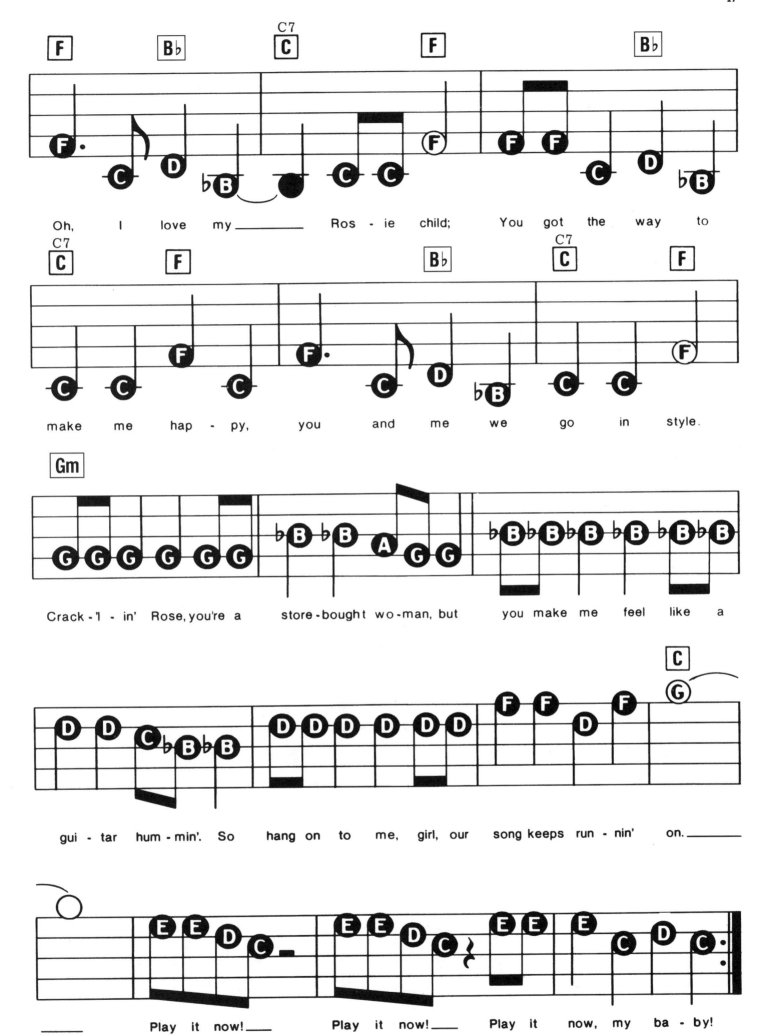

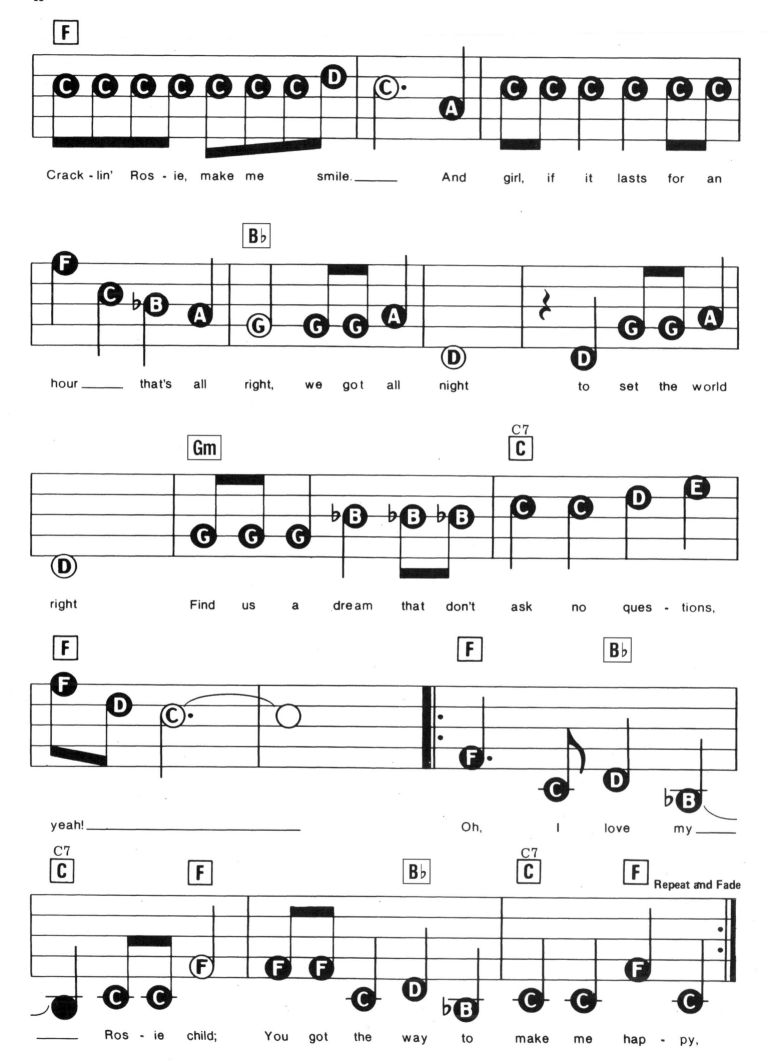

Defying Gravity
from the Broadway Musical WICKED

Registration 7
Rhythm: Pop or Rock

Music and Lyrics by
Stephen Schwartz

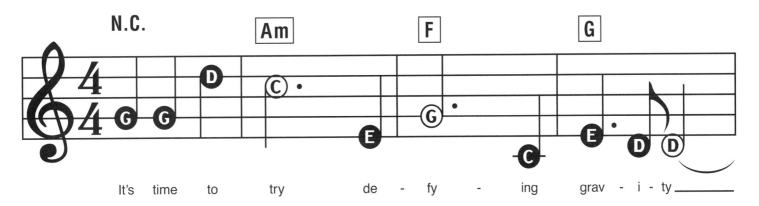

It's time to try de - fy - ing grav - i - ty _____

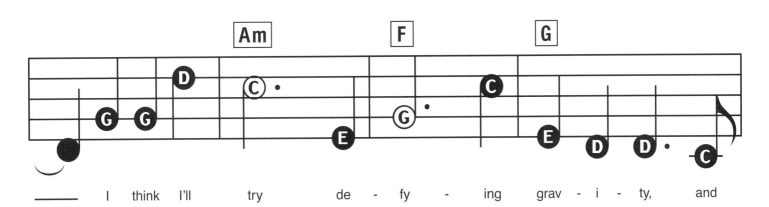

_____ I think I'll try de - fy - ing grav - i - ty, and

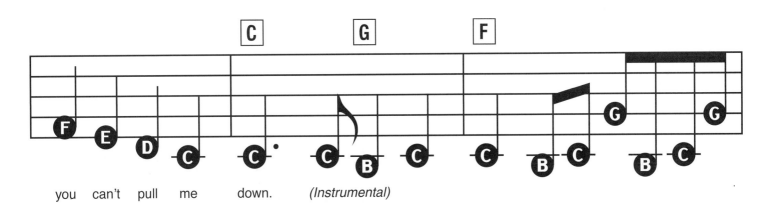

you can't pull me down. *(Instrumental)*

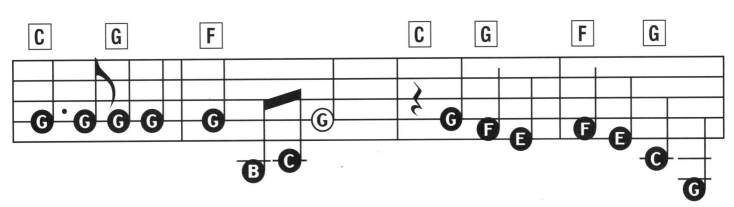

I'm through ac - cept - ing lim - its

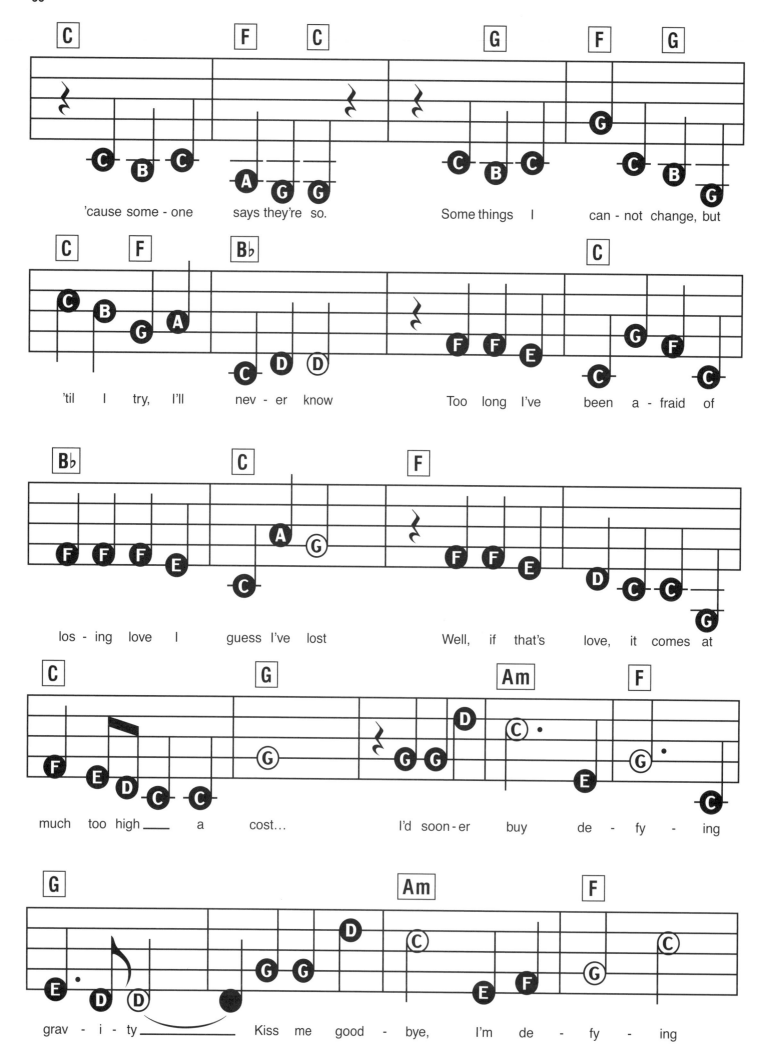

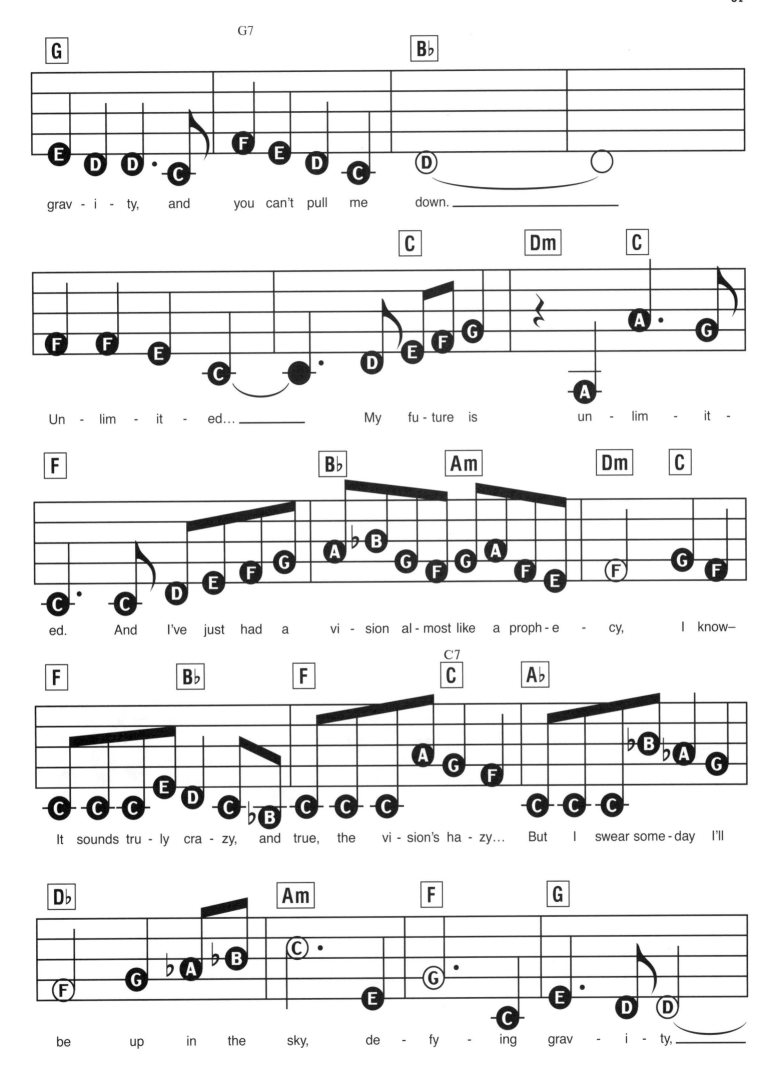

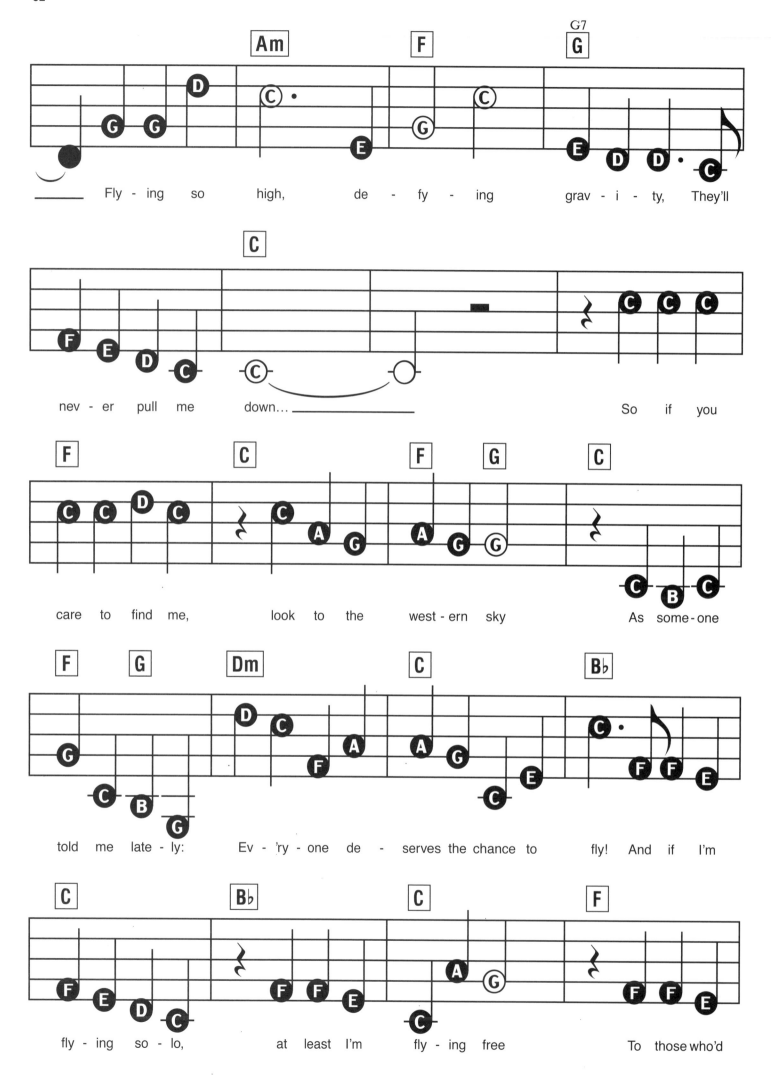

52

53

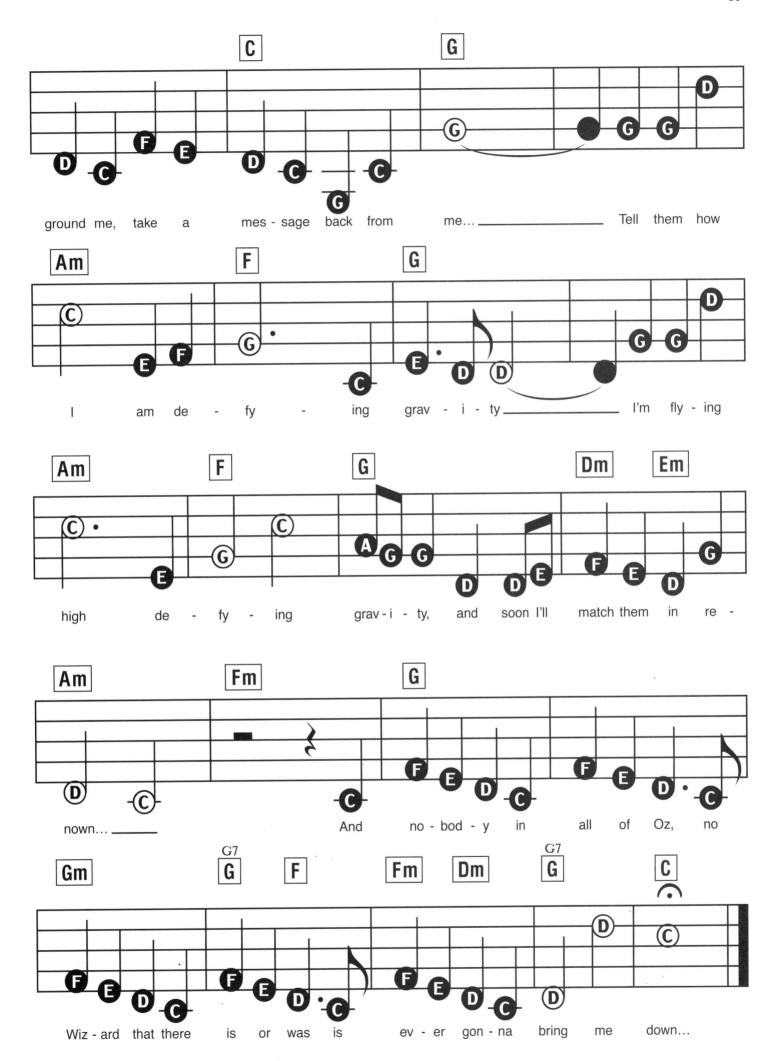

Crazy

Registration 2
Rhythm: Country or Ballad

Words and Music by
Willie Nelson

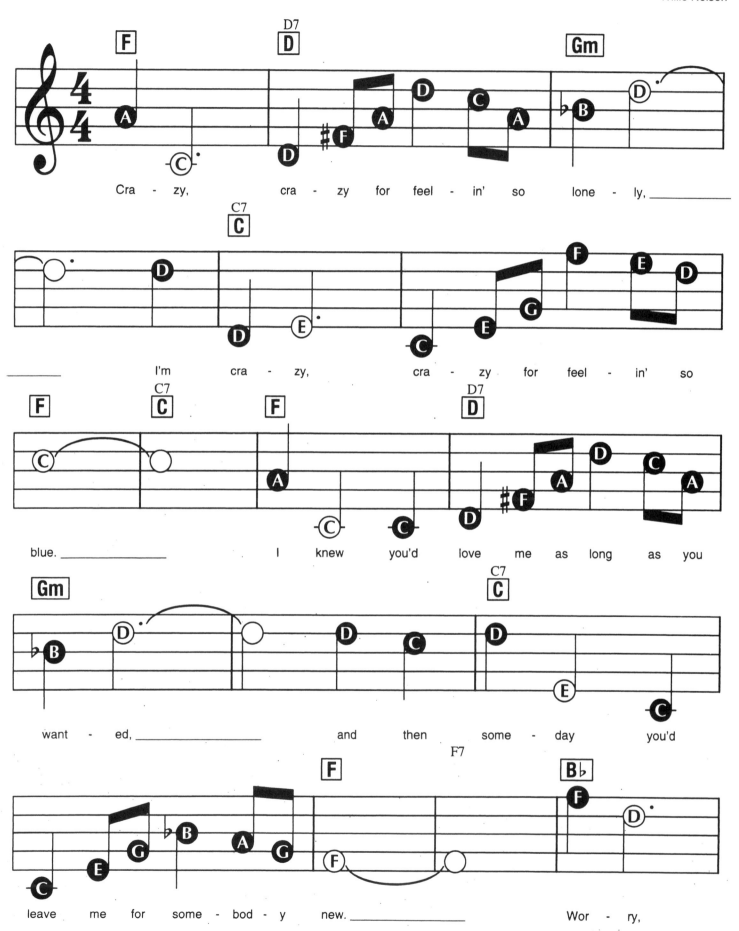

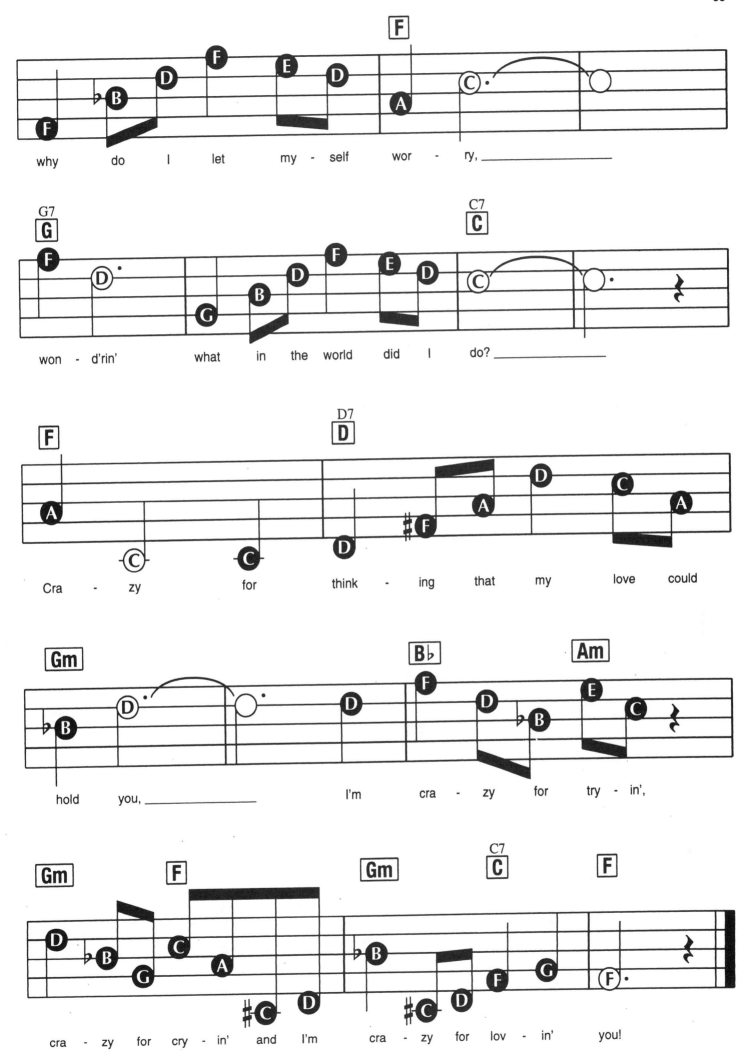

Feeling Good

from THE ROAR OF THE GREASEPAINT – THE SMELL OF THE CROWD

Registration 8
Rhythm: 4/4 Ballad or Rock

Words and Music by Leslie Bricusse
and Anthony Newley

Bird fly - ing high, you know how I feel.
Fish in the sea, you know how I feel.

Sun in the sky, you know how I feel. Breeze drift - ing by,
Riv - er run - ning free, you know how I feel. Blos - som on the tree,

you know how I feel.
you know how I feel. It's a new dawn, it's a new day, it's a

new life _____ for _____ me, _____ feel - ing good. _____

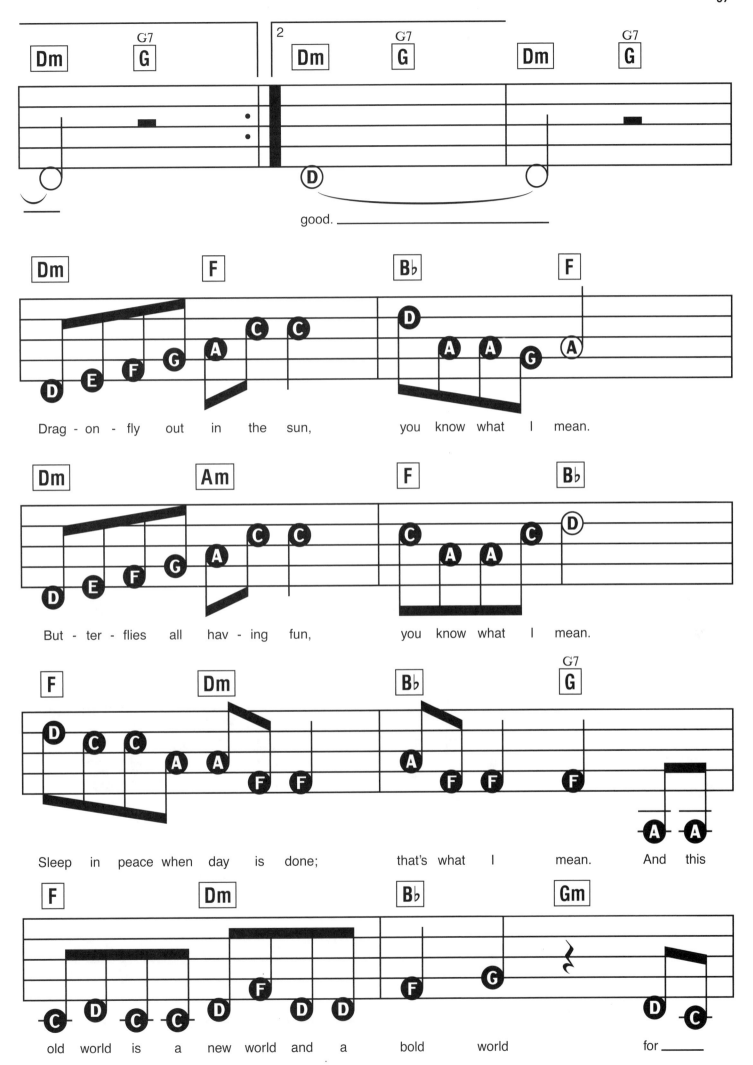

58

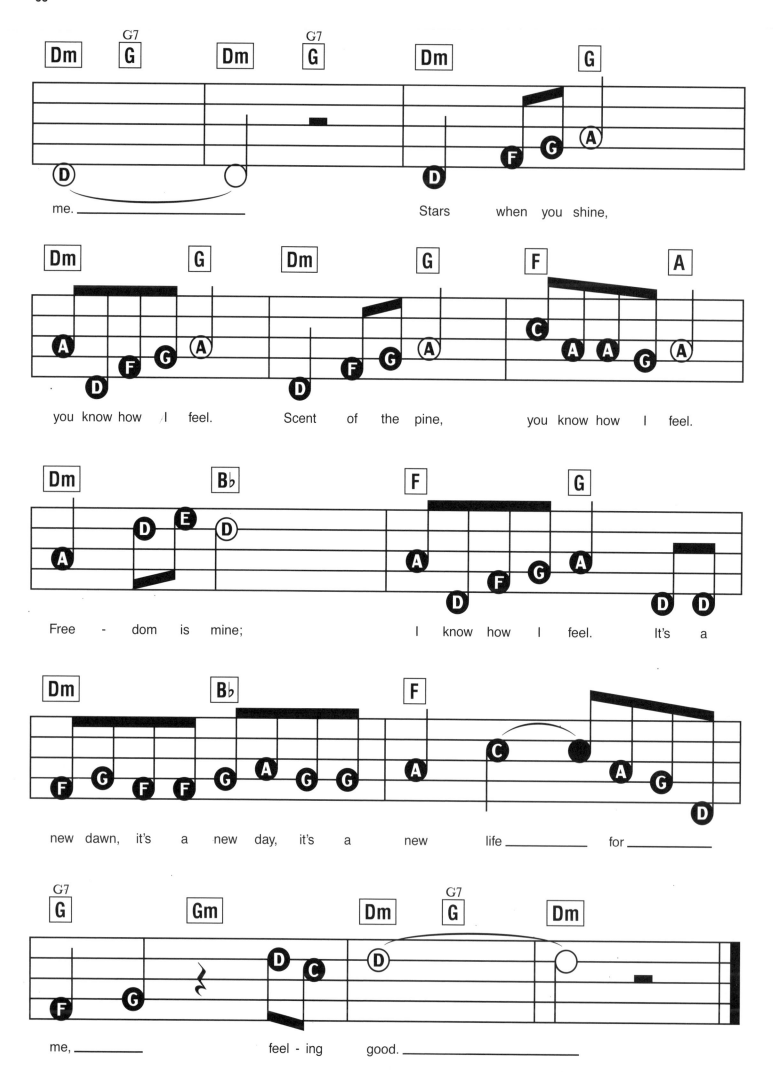

Flip, Flop and Fly

Registration 2
Rhythm: Shuffle or Rock

Words and Music by Charles Calhoun
and Lou Willie Turner

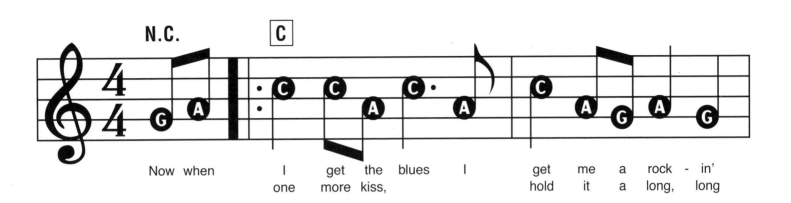

Now when I get the blues I get me a rock-in'
one more kiss, hold it a long, long

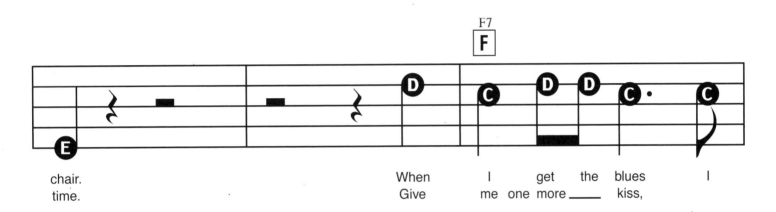

chair. When I get the blues I
time. Give me one more ____ kiss,

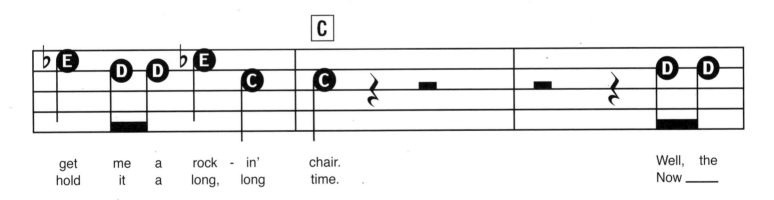

get me a rock-in' chair. Well, the
hold it a long, long time. Now ____

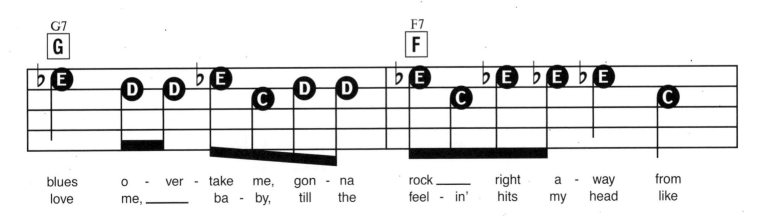

blues o-ver-take me, gon-na rock ____ right a-way from
love me, ____ ba-by, till the feel-in' hits my head like

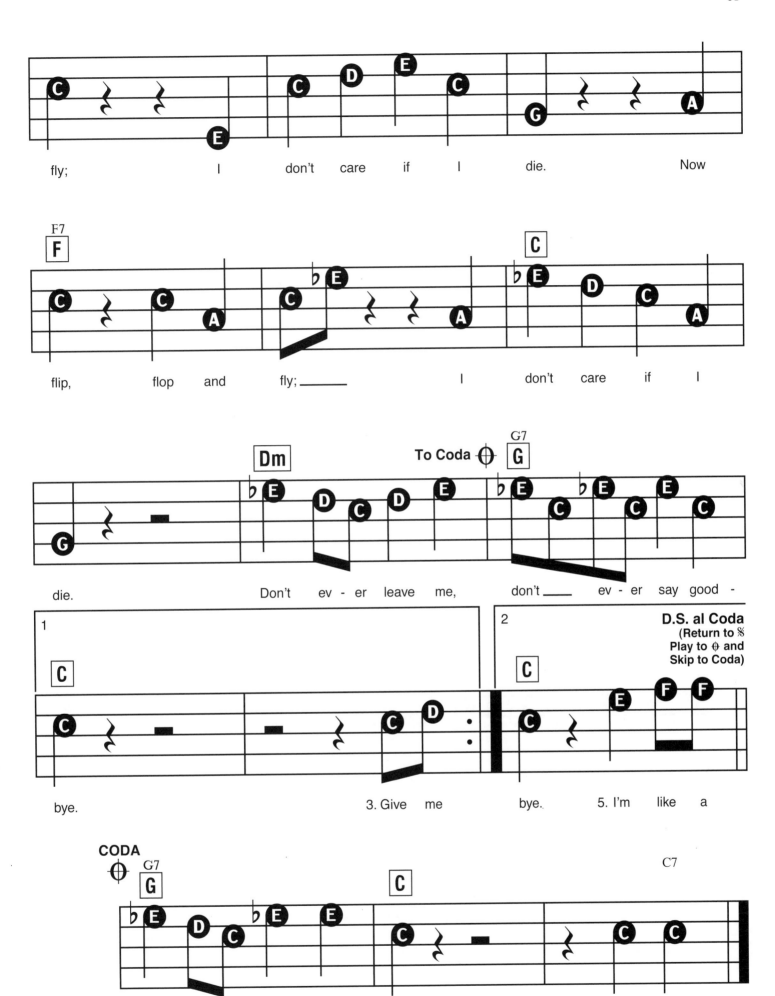

Fields of Gold

Registration 4
Rhythm: Rock or 8-Beat

Music and Lyrics by
Sting

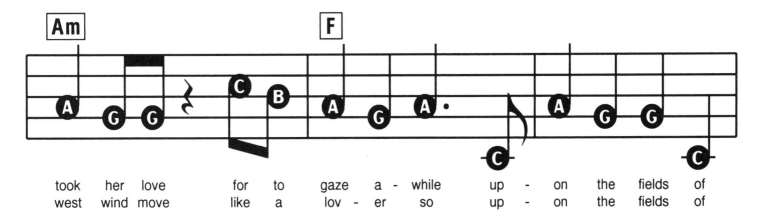

took her love for to gaze a - while up - on the fields of
west wind move like a lov - er so up - on the fields of

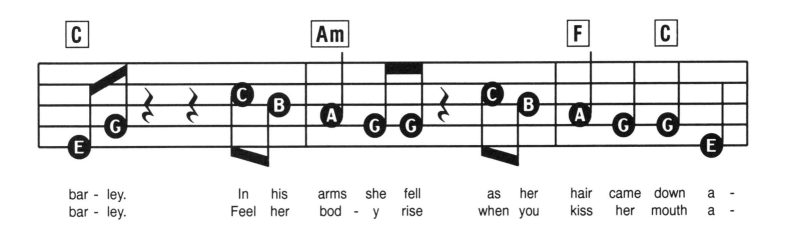

bar - ley. In his arms she fell as her hair came down a -
bar - ley. Feel her bod - y rise when you kiss her mouth a -

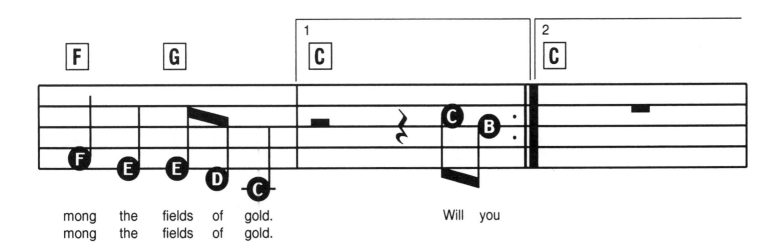

mong the fields of gold. Will you
mong the fields of gold.

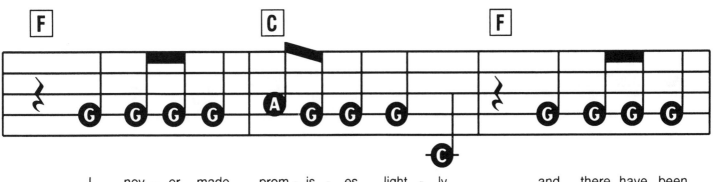

I nev - er made prom - is - es light - ly and there have been

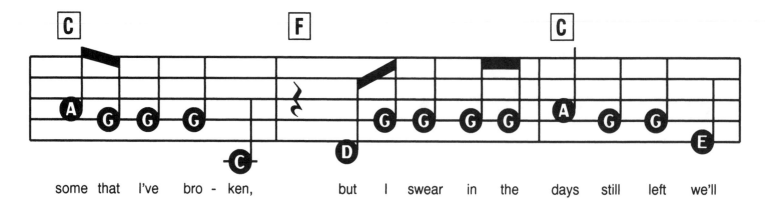

some that I've bro - ken,   but I swear in the days still left we'll

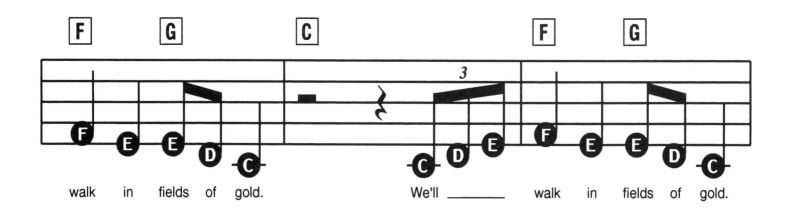

walk in fields of gold.   We'll _____ walk in fields of gold.

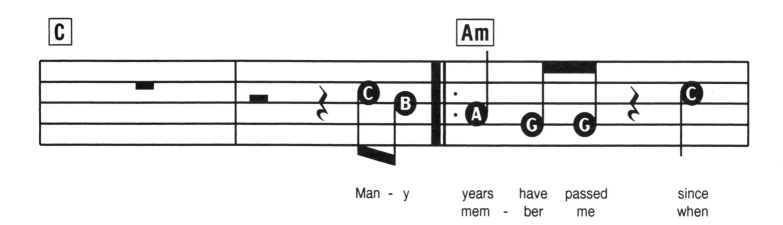

Man - y years have passed since
mem - ber me when

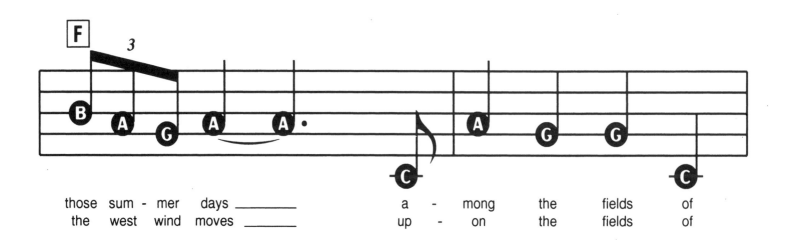

those sum - mer days _____ a - mong the fields of
the west wind moves _____ up - on the fields of

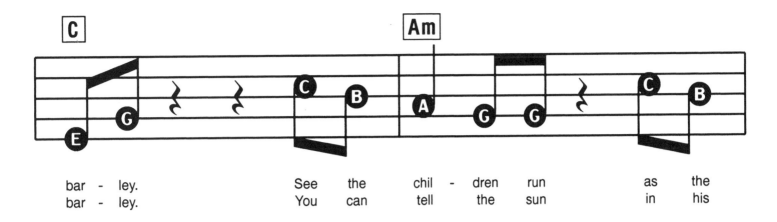

bar - ley.   See   the   chil - dren   run   as   the
bar - ley.   You   can   tell   the   sun   in   his

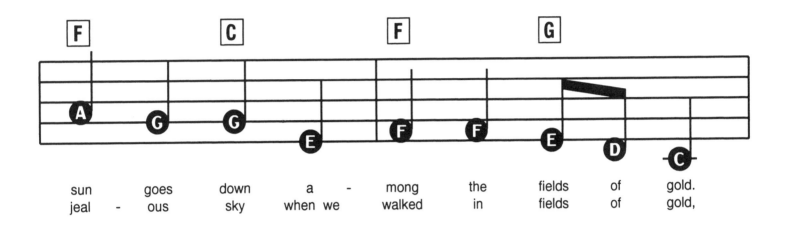

sun   goes   down   a -   mong   the   fields   of   gold.
jeal - ous   sky   when we   walked   in   fields   of   gold,

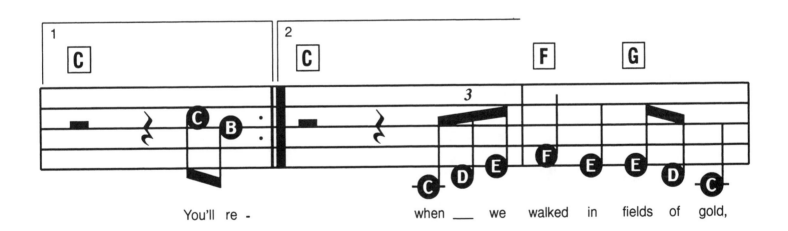

You'll re -   when ___ we   walked   in   fields   of   gold,

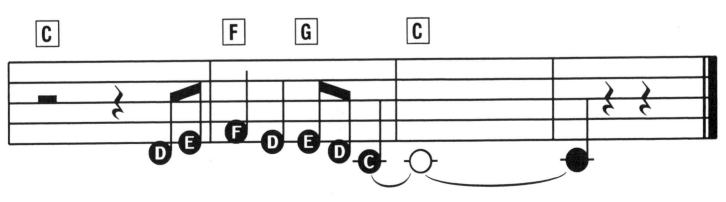

when we   walked   in   fields   of   gold. _____

Fly Me to the Moon
(In Other Words)

Registration 2
Rhythm: Waltz or Jazz Waltz

Words and Music by
Bart Howard

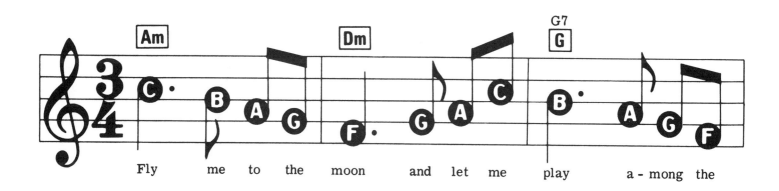

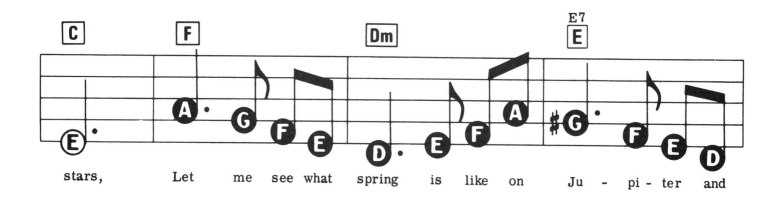

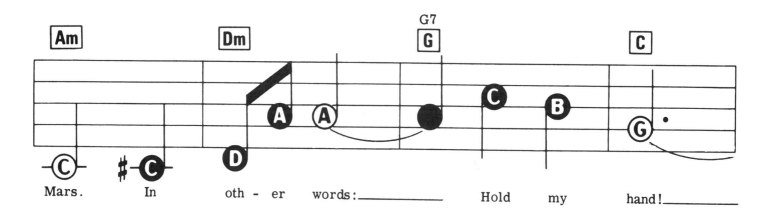

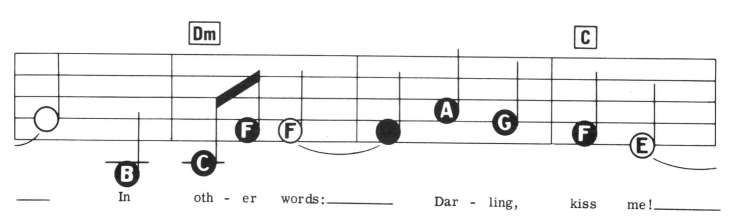

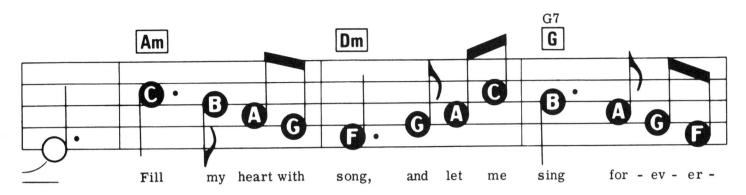

Fill my heart with song, and let me sing for - ev - er -

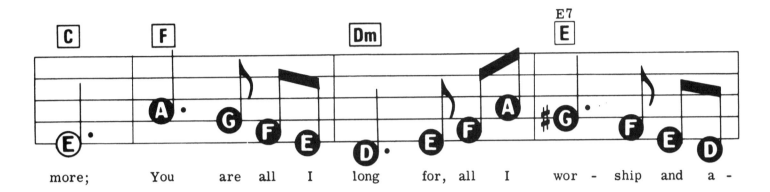

more; You are all I long for, all I wor - ship and a -

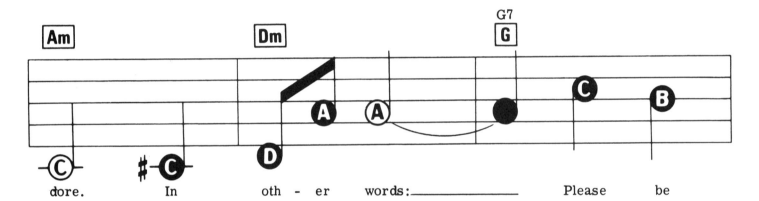

dore. In oth - er words:_____ Please be

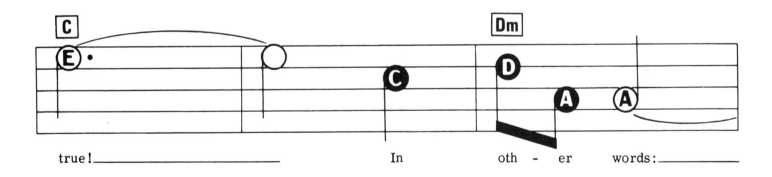

true!_____ In oth - er words:_____

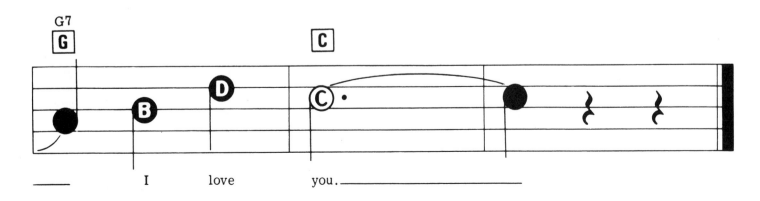

I love you._____

Hallelujah

Registration 4
Rhythm: 6/8 March

Words and Music by
Leonard Cohen

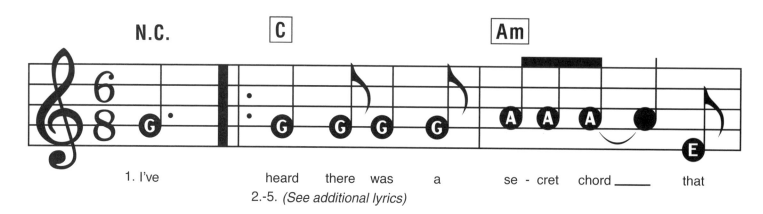

1. I've heard there was a se - cret chord _____ that
2.-5. *(See additional lyrics)*

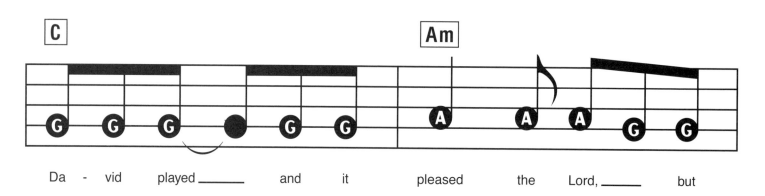

Da - vid played _____ and it pleased the Lord, _____ but

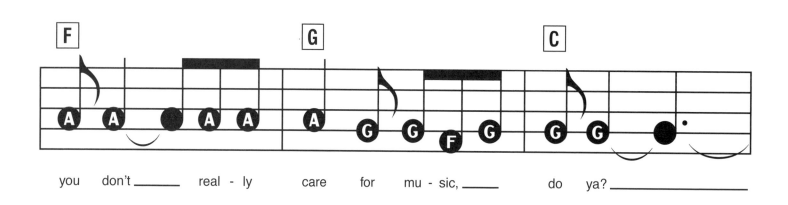

you don't _____ real - ly care for mu - sic, _____ do ya? _____

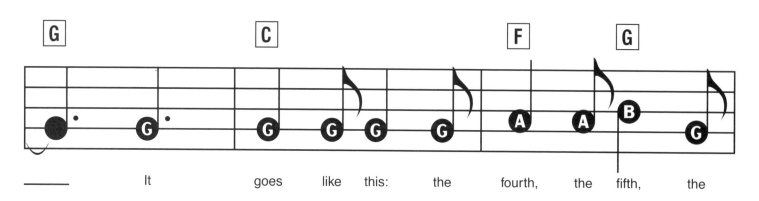

_____ It goes like this: the fourth, the fifth, the

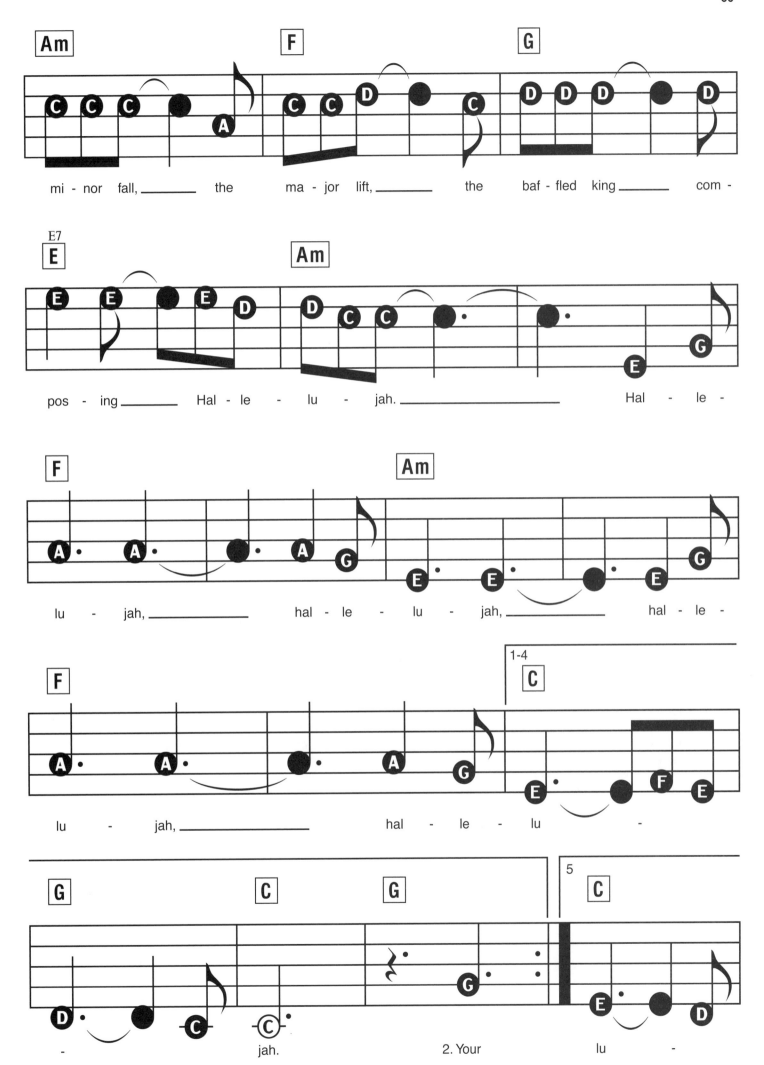

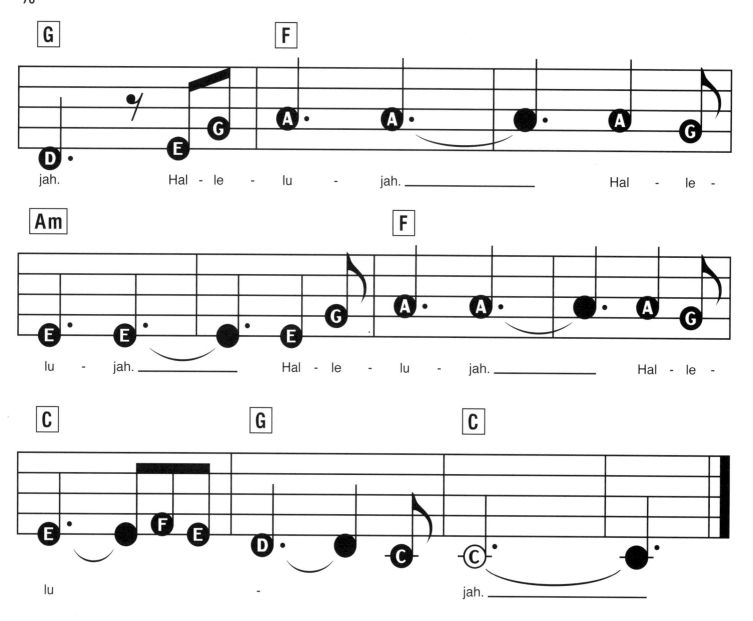

Additional Lyrics

2. Your faith was strong but you needed proof.
   You saw her bathing on the roof.
   Her beauty and the moonlight overthrew ya.
   She tied you to a kitchen chair.
   She broke your throne, she cut your hair.
   And from your lips she drew the Hallelujah.

3. Maybe I have been here before.
   I know this room, I've walked this floor.
   I used to live alone before I knew ya.
   I've seen your flag on the marble arch.
   Love is not a vict'ry march.
   It's a cold and it's a broken Hallelujah.

4. There was a time you let me know
   What's real and going on below.
   But now you never show it to me, do ya?
   And remember when I moved in you.
   The holy dark was movin', too,
   And every breath we drew was Hallelujah.

5. Maybe there's a God above,
   And all I ever learned from love
   Was how to shoot at someone who outdrew ya.
   And it's not a cry you can hear at night.
   It's not somebody who's seen the light.
   It's a cold and it's a broken Hallelujah.

Free Bird

Registration 2
Rhythm: Slow Rock or 8-Beat

Words and Music by Allen Collins
and Ronnie Van Zant

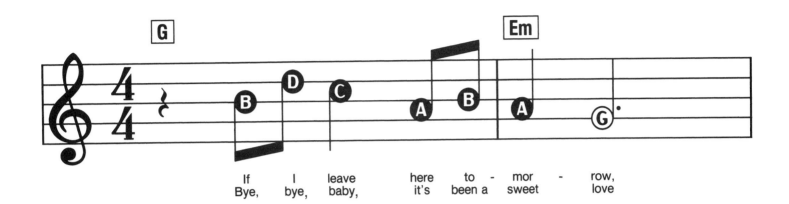

If   I   leave   here   to - mor - row,
Bye,   bye,   baby,   it's   been a   sweet   love

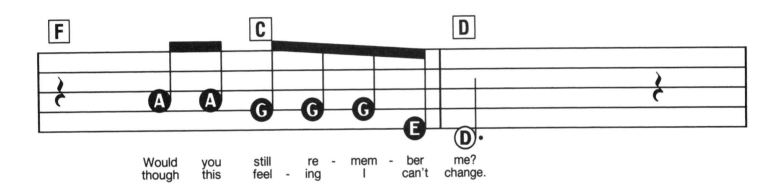

Would   you   still   re - mem - ber   me?
though   this   feel - ing   I   can't   change.

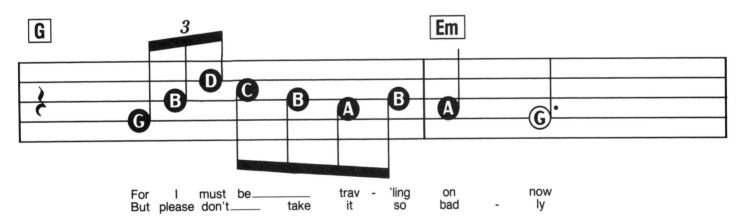

For   I   must   be_____   trav - 'ling   on   now
But   please   don't_____   take   it   so   bad - ly

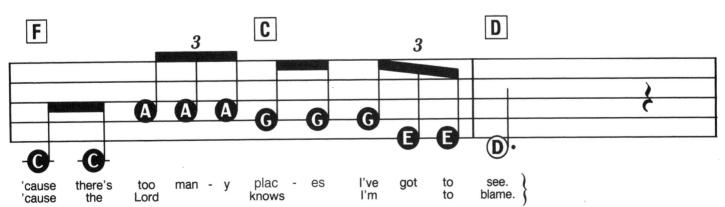

'cause   there's   too   man - y   plac - es   I've   got   to   see.
'cause   the   Lord   knows   I'm   to   blame.

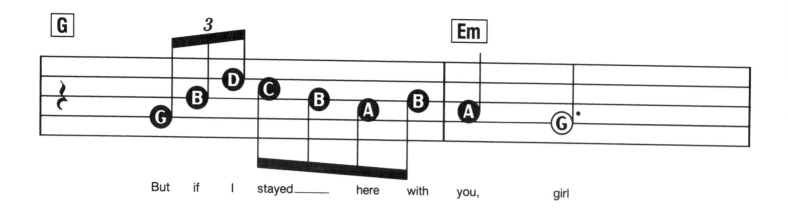

But if I stayed_____ here with you, girl

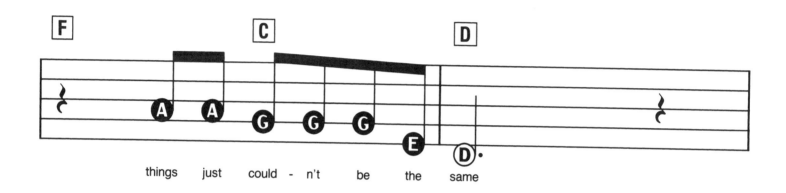

things just could - n't be the same

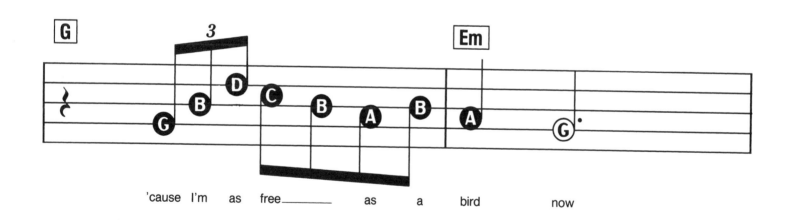

'cause I'm as free_____ as a bird now

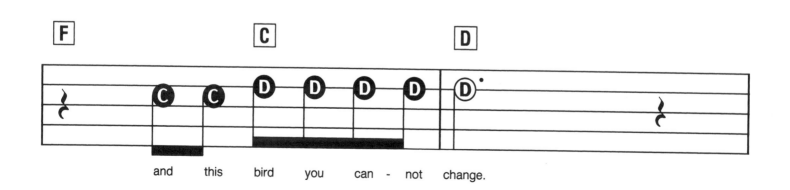

and this bird you can - not change.

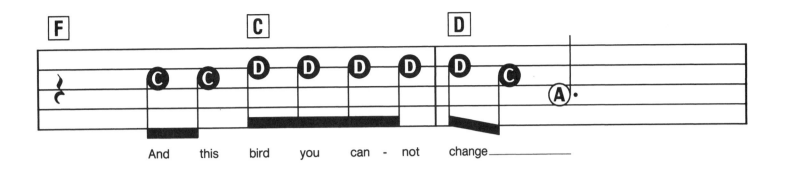

And this bird you can - not change_____

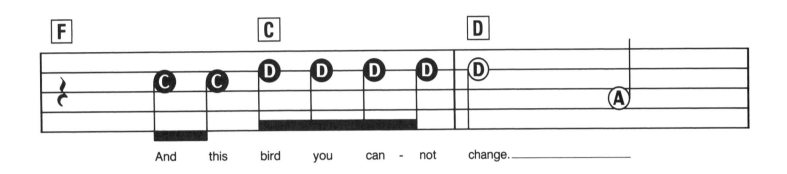

And this bird you can - not change._____

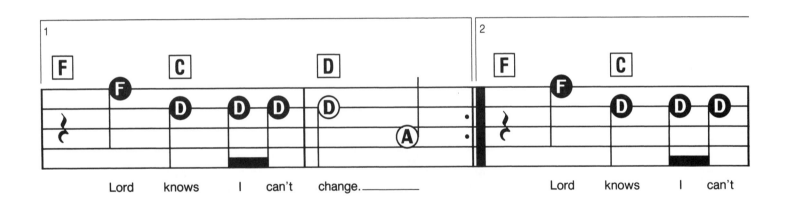

Lord knows I can't change._____

Lord knows I can't

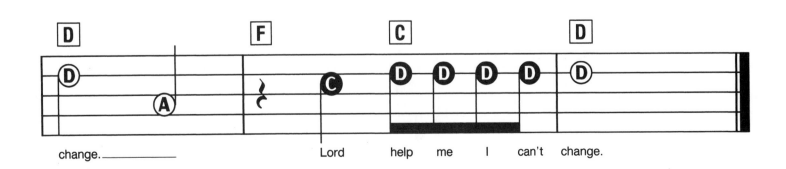

change._____ Lord help me I can't change.

The Frim Fram Sauce

Registration 2
Rhythm: Swing

Words and Music by Joe Ricardel
and Redd Evans

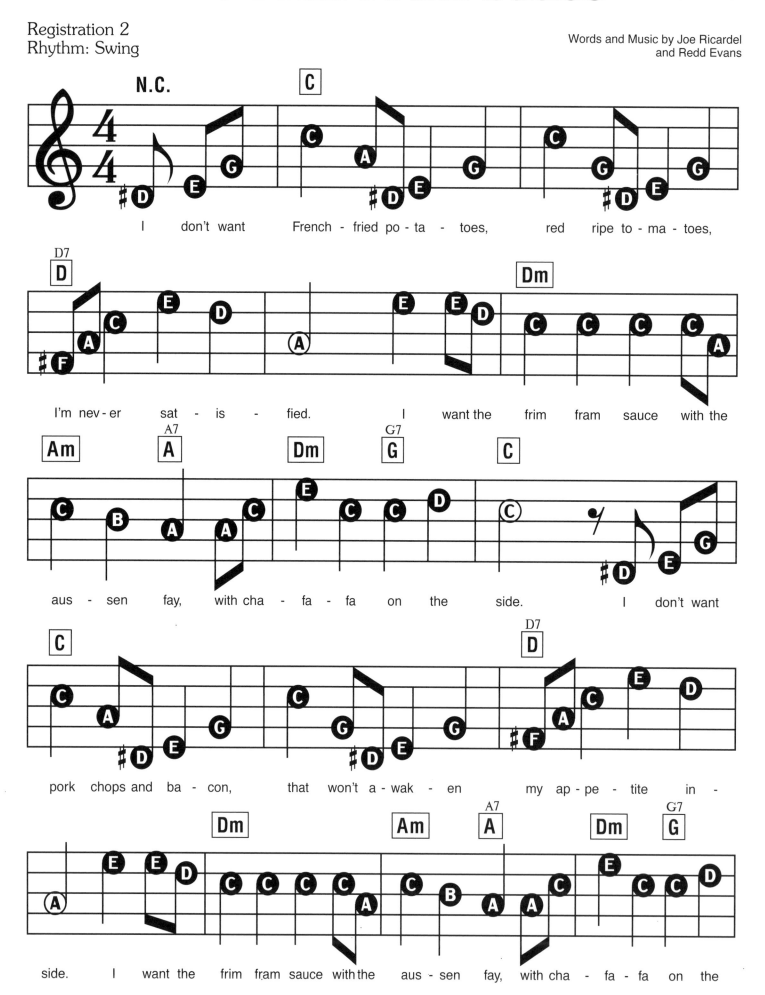

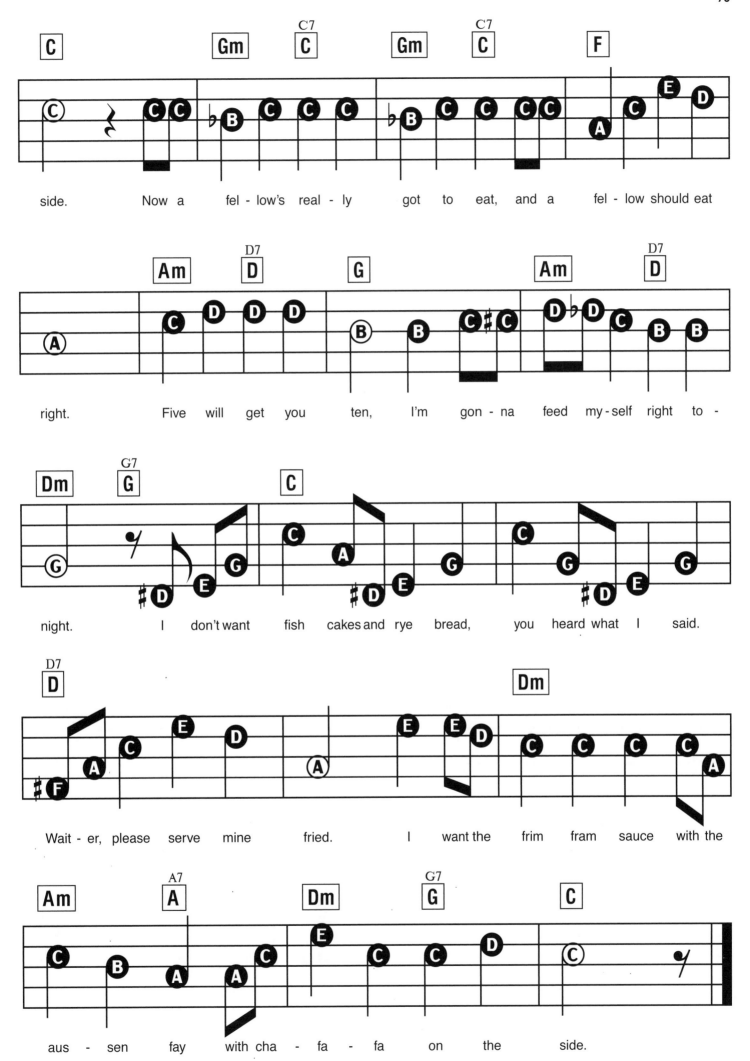

Gentle Rain
from the Motion Picture THE GENTLE RAIN

Registration 4
Rhythm: Bossa Nova or Latin

Music by Luiz Bonfa
Words by Matt Dubey

We — both are lost and a - lone in the
I — feel your tears as they fall on my

world, — walk with me _____ in the gen - tle
cheek, — they are warm _____ like the gen - tle

rain. _____
rain. _____ Don't — be a -
Come, — lit - tle

fraid, — I've a hand for your hand, — and I
one, — you have me in the world. And our

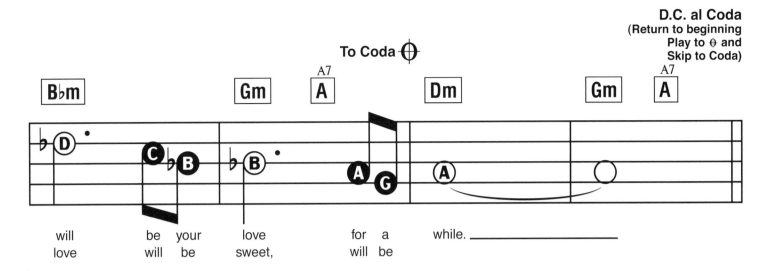

D.C. al Coda
(Return to beginning
Play to ⊕ and
Skip to Coda)

To Coda ⊕

will
love
be your
will be
love
sweet,
for a
will be
while. _____

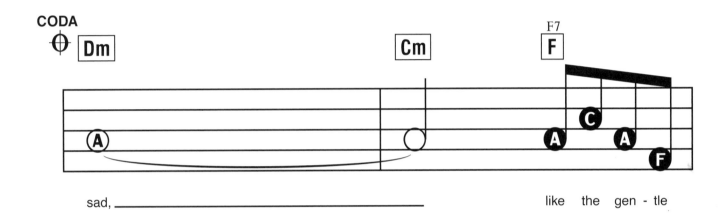

CODA ⊕

sad, _____ like the gen - tle

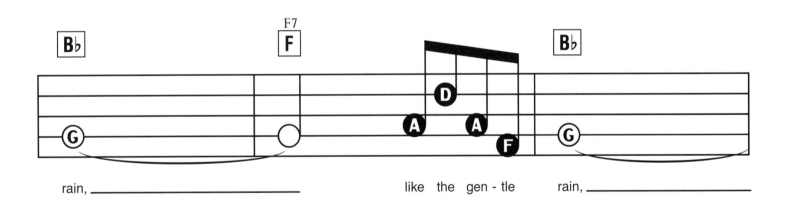

rain, _____ like the gen - tle rain, _____

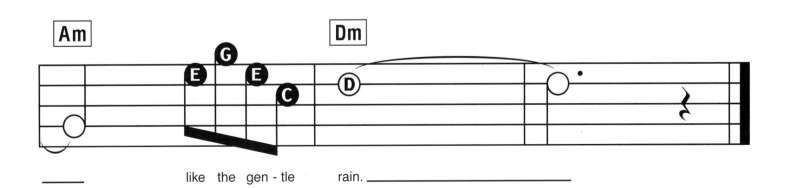

_____ like the gen - tle rain. _____

Georgia on My Mind

Registration 4
Rhythm: Swing or Ballad

Words by Stuart Gorrell
Music by Hoagy Carmichael

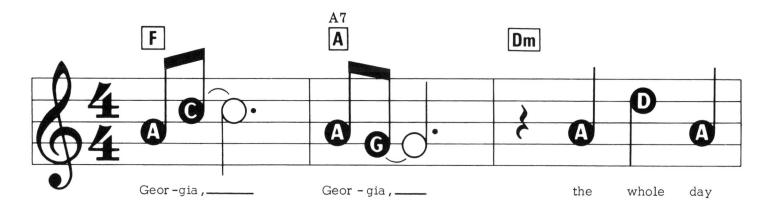

Geor-gia,_____ Geor-gia,_____ the whole day

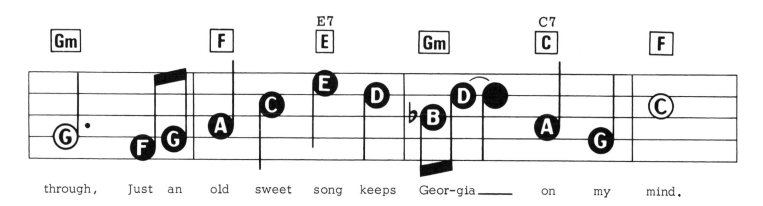

through, Just an old sweet song keeps Geor-gia_____ on my mind.

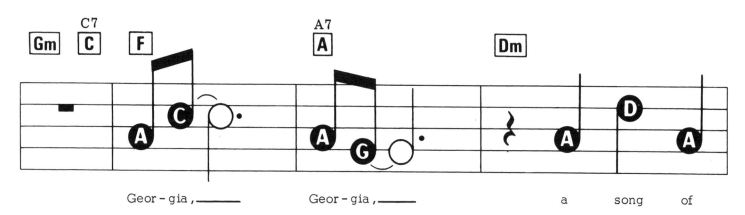

Geor-gia,_____ Geor-gia,_____ a song of

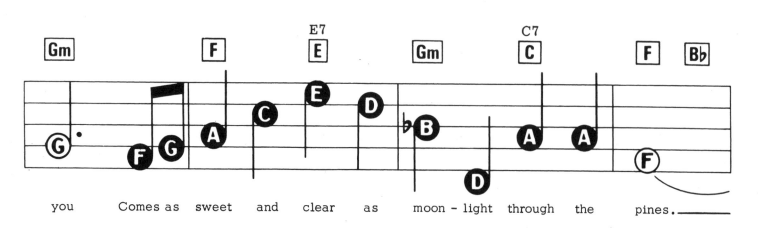

you Comes as sweet and clear as moon-light through the pines._____

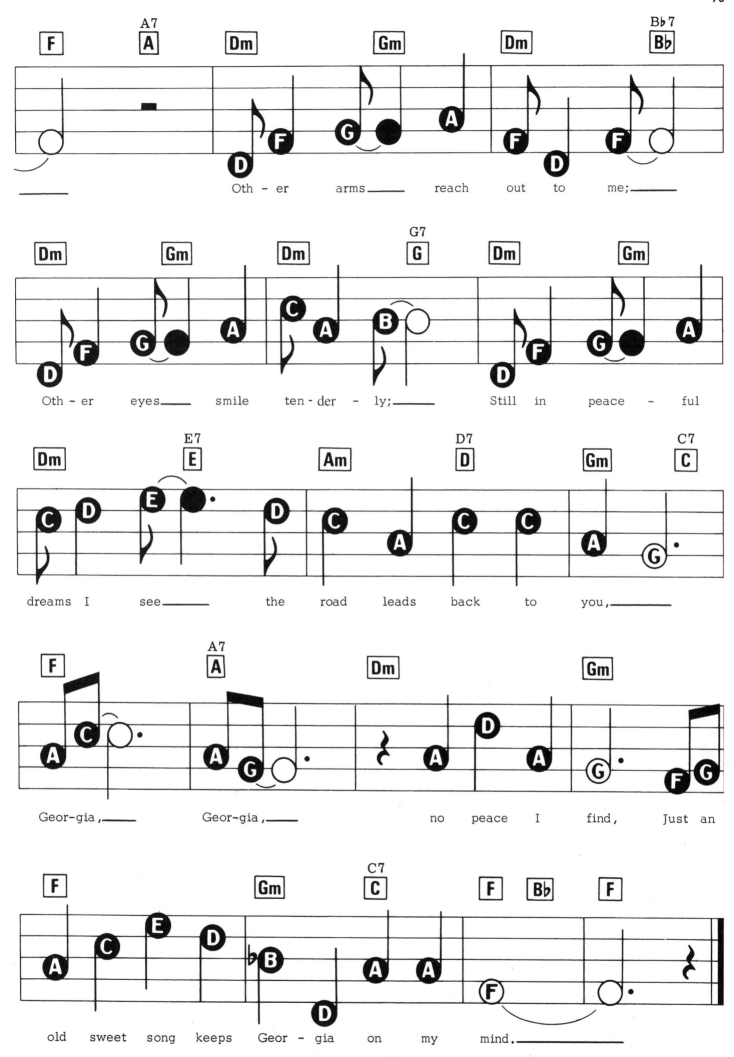

Hey Jude

Registration 2
Rhythm: Pops or 8-Beat

Words and Music by John Lennon
and Paul McCartney

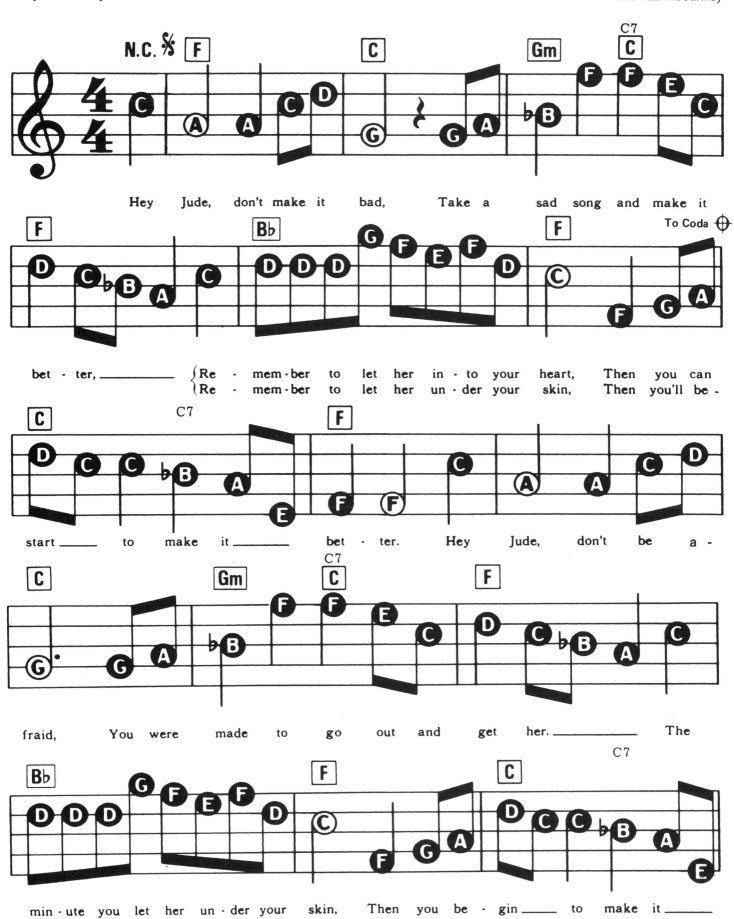

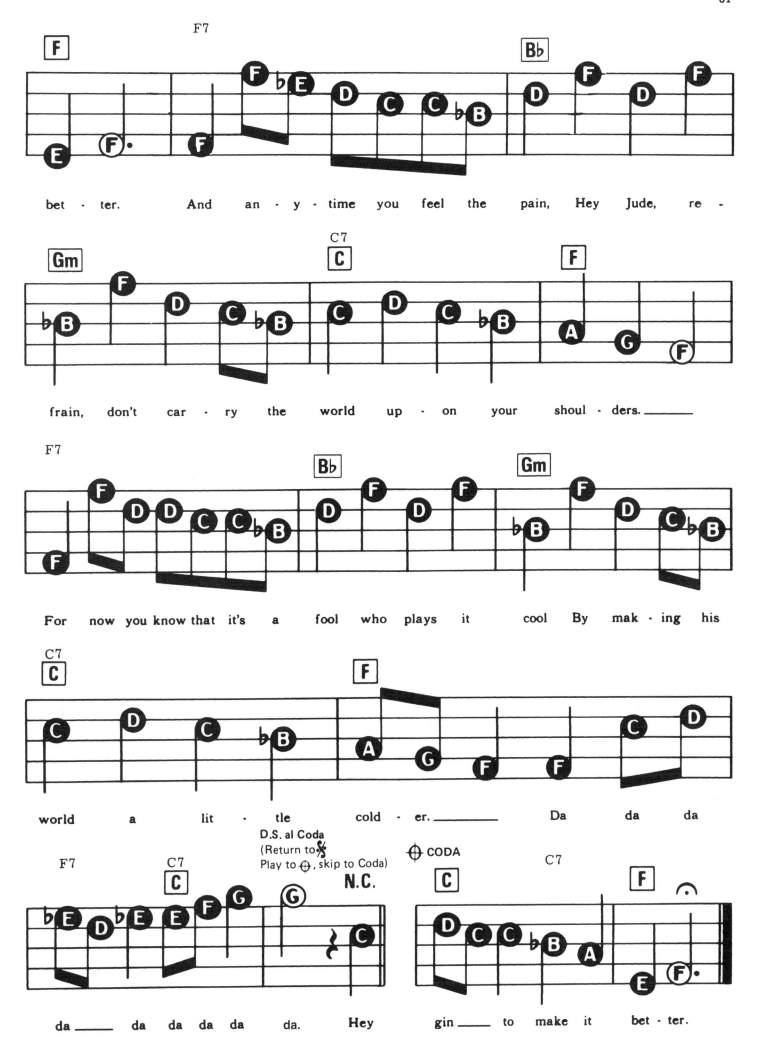

Hotel California

Registration 9
Rhythm: Rock or Disco

Words and Music by Don Henley,
Glenn Frey and Don Felder

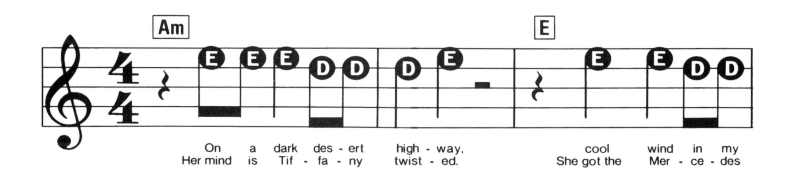

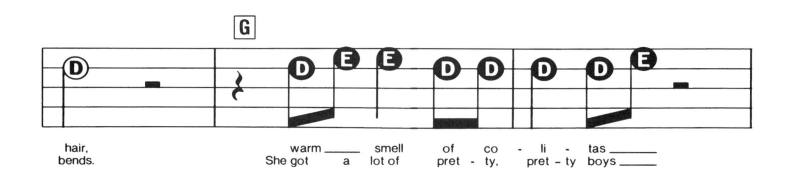

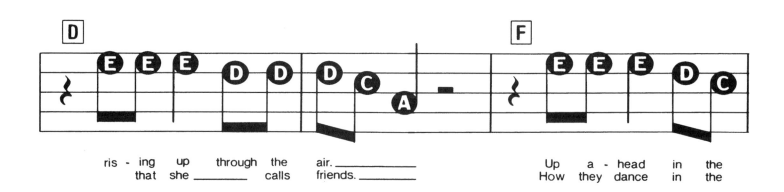

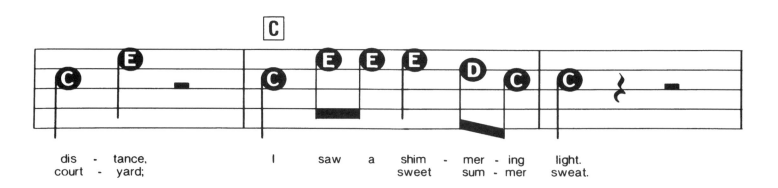

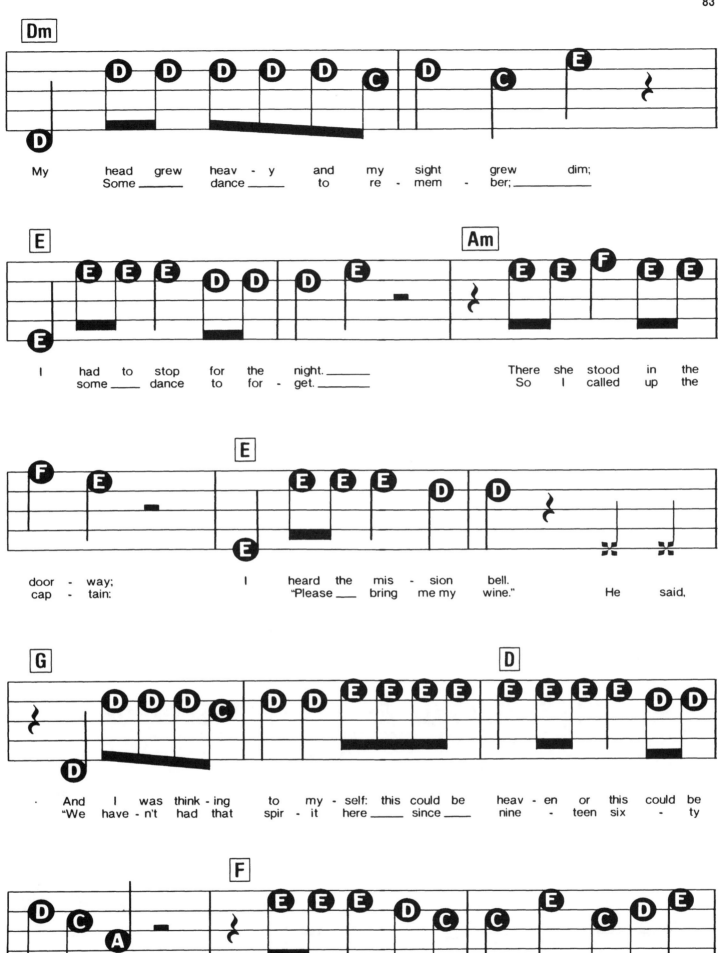

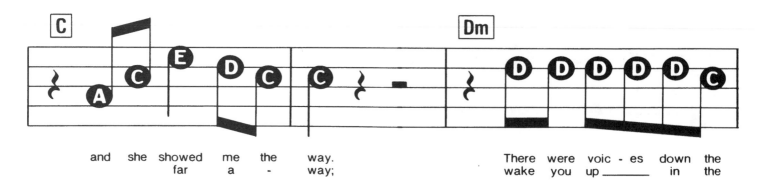

and she showed me the way.
far a - way;
There were voic - es down the
wake you up _____ in the

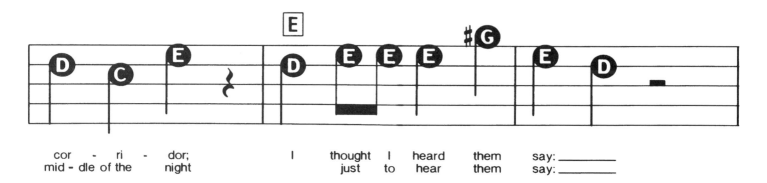

cor - ri - dor;
mid - dle of the night
I thought I heard them say: _____
just to hear them say: _____

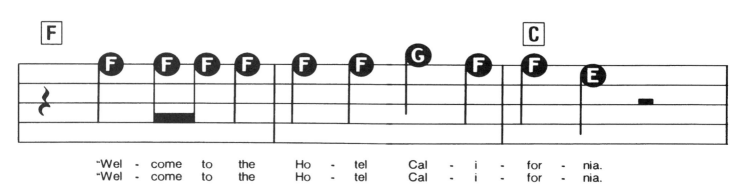

"Wel - come to the Ho - tel Cal - i - for - nia.
"Wel - come to the Ho - tel Cal - i - for - nia.

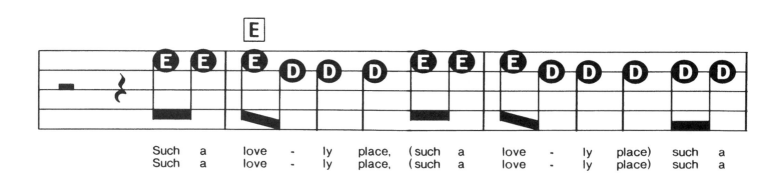

Such a love - ly place, (such a love - ly place) such a
Such a love - ly place, (such a love - ly place) such a

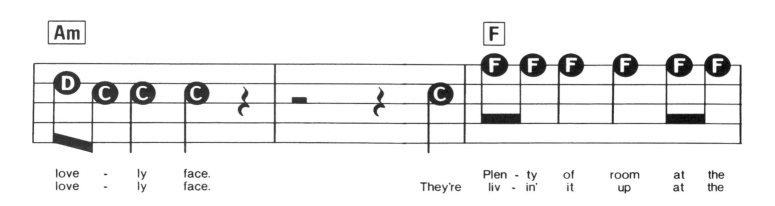

love - ly face.
love - ly face.
Plen - ty of room at the
They're liv - in' it up at the

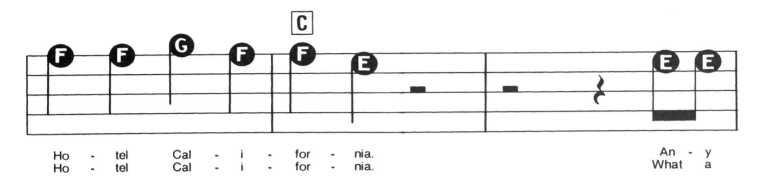

Ho - tel Cal - i - for - nia. An - y
Ho - tel Cal - i - for - nia. What a

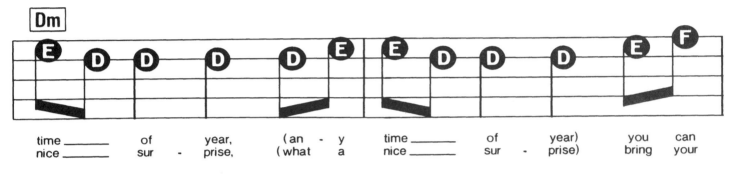

time _____ of year, (an - y time _____ of year) you can
nice _____ sur - prise, (what a nice _____ sur - prise) you can

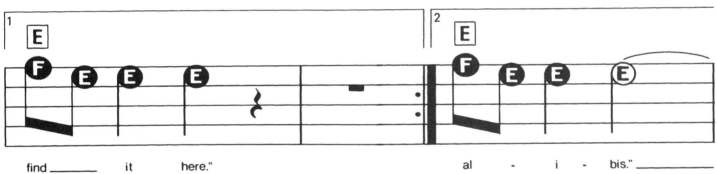

find _____ it here." al - i - bis." _____

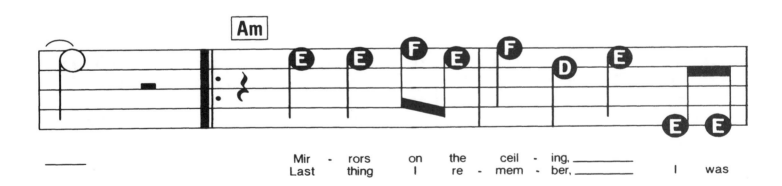

_____ Mir - rors on the ceil - ing, _____
Last thing I re - mem - ber, _____ I was

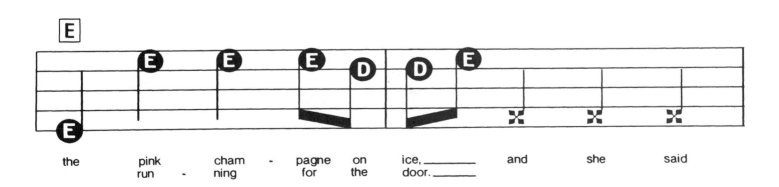

the pink cham - pagne on ice, _____ and she said
run - ning for the door. _____

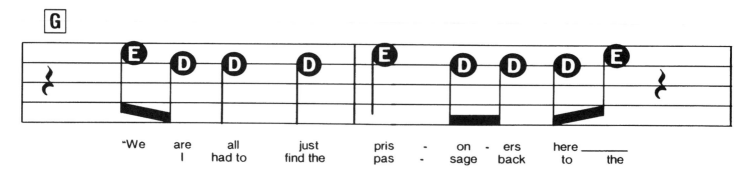

"We are all just pris - on - ers here _____
I had to just find the pas - sage back to the

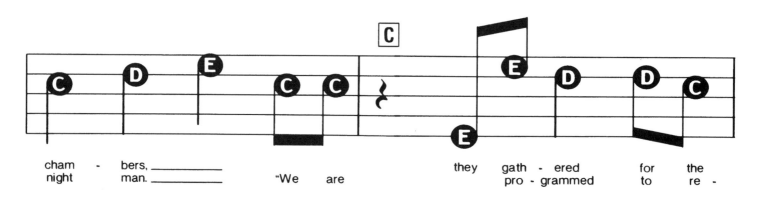

of our own _____ de - vice." And in the mas - ter's _____
place I was _____ be - fore. "Re - lax," said the

cham - bers, _____ they gath - ered for the
night man. _____ "We are pro - grammed to re -

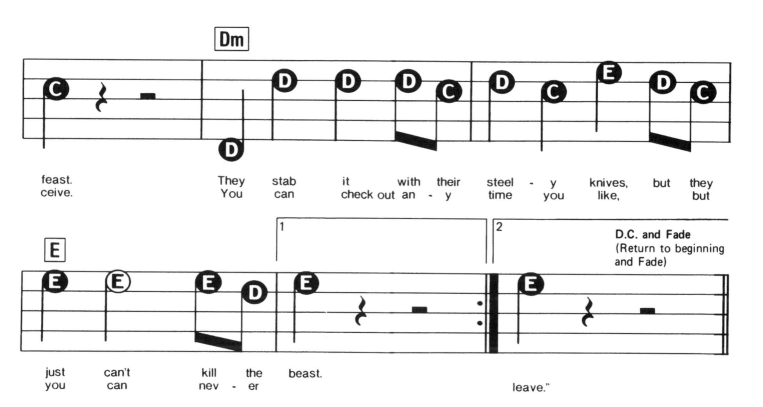

feast. They stab it with their steel - y knives, but they
ceive. You can check out an - y time you like, but

D.C. and Fade
(Return to beginning and Fade)

just can't kill the beast.
you can nev - er leave."

It Had to Be You

Registration 9
Rhythm: Swing

Words by Gus Kahn
Music by Isham Jones

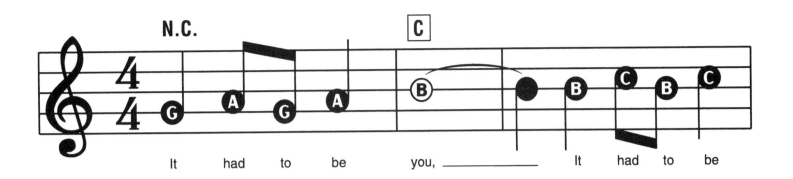

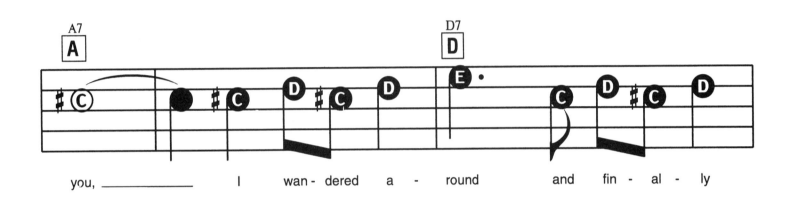

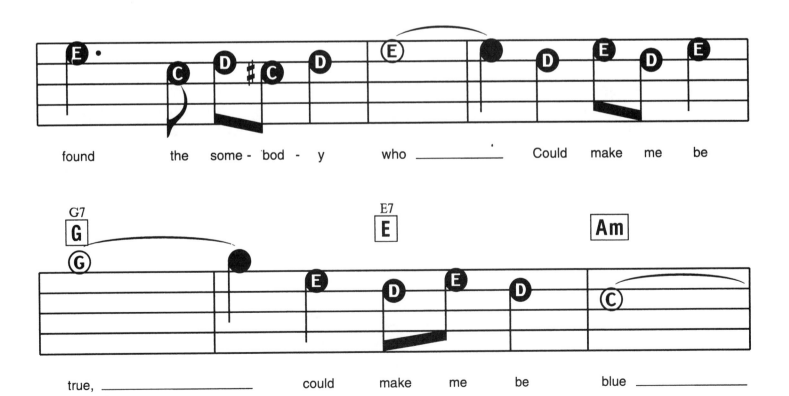

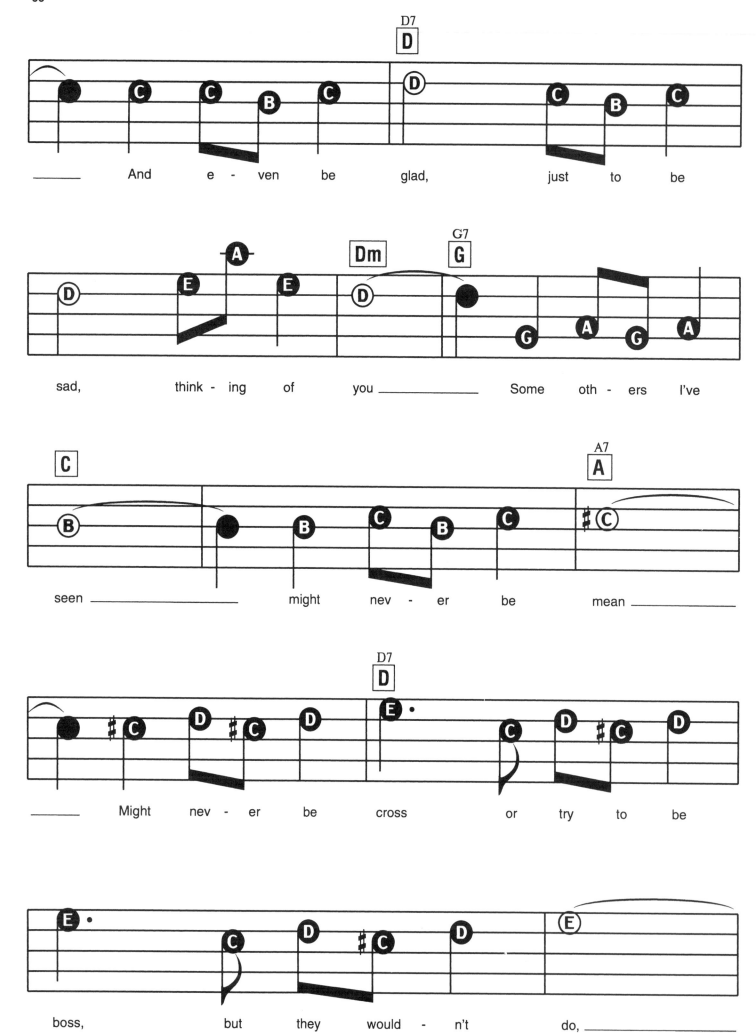

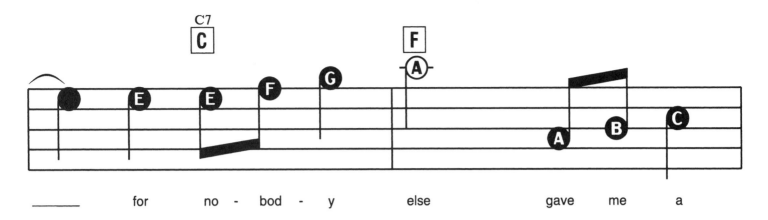

_____ for no - bod - y else gave me a

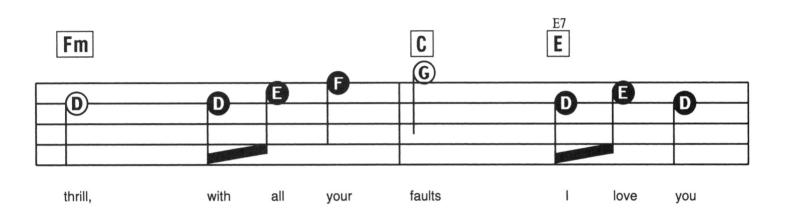

thrill, with all your faults I love you

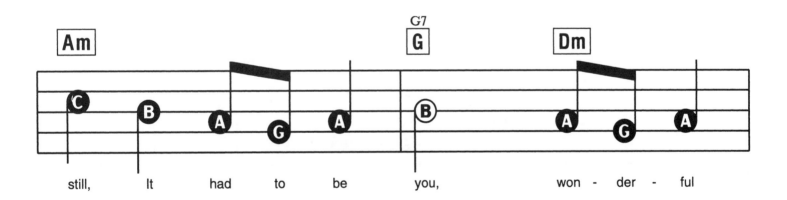

still, It had to be you, won - der - ful

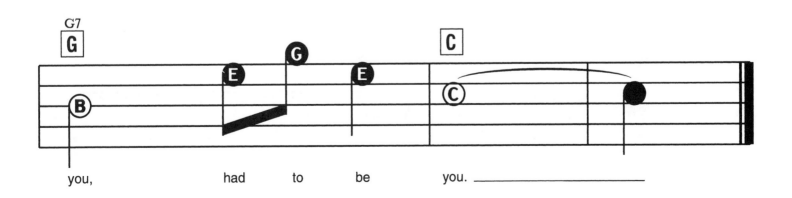

you, had to be you. _____

I Have a Dream
from MAMMA MIA!

Registration 3
Rhythm: Ballad

Words and Music by Benny Andersson
and Bjorn Ulvaeus

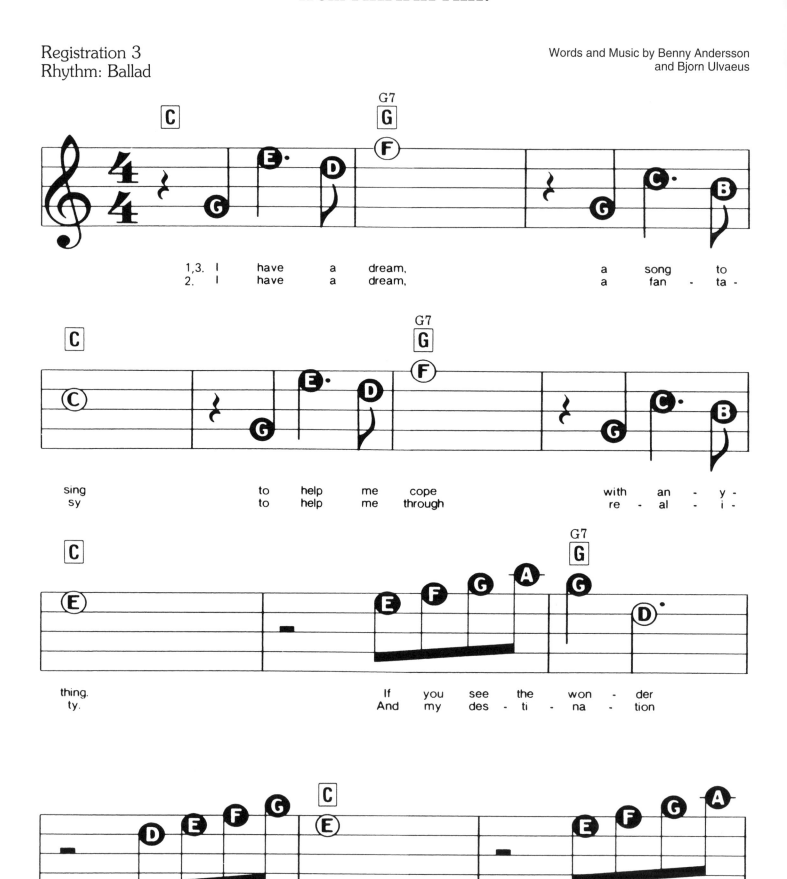

1,3. I have a dream, a song to
2. I have a dream, a fan - ta -

sing to help me cope with an - y -
sy to help me through re - al - i -

thing. If you see the won - der
ty. And my des - ti - na - tion

of a fair - y tale, you can take the
makes it worth the while, push - ing through the

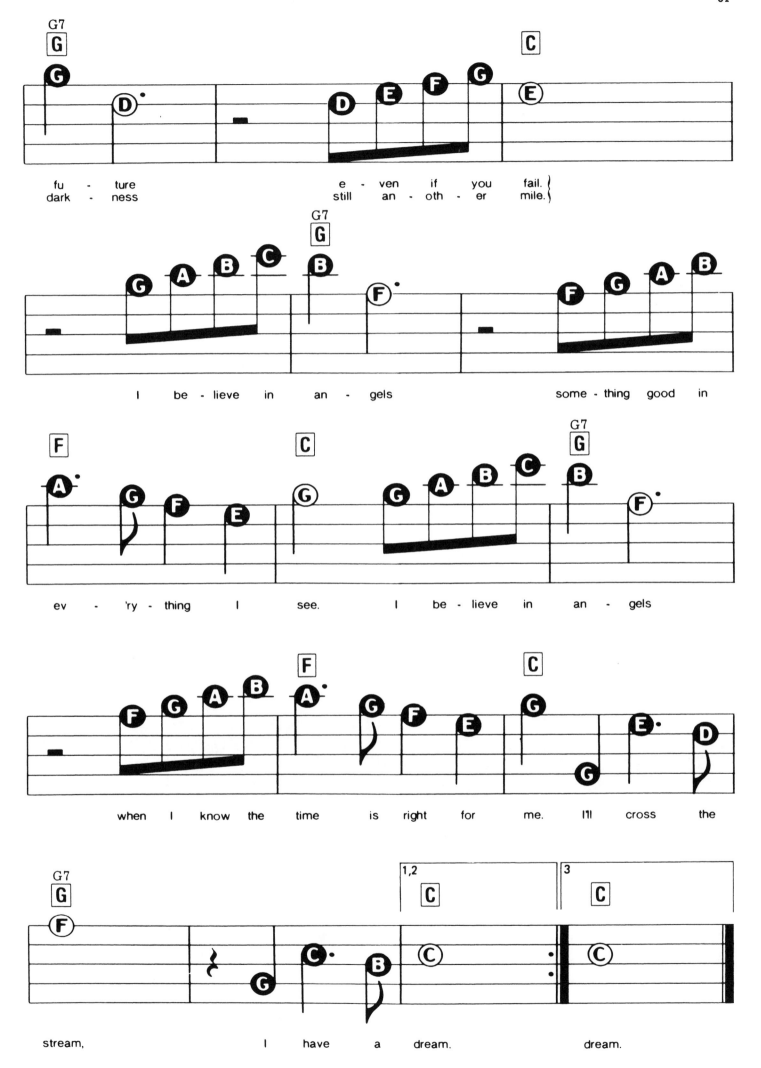

91

I Only Have Eyes for You
from DAMES

Registration 3
Rhythm: Fox Trot or Swing

Words by Al Dubin
Music by Harry Warren

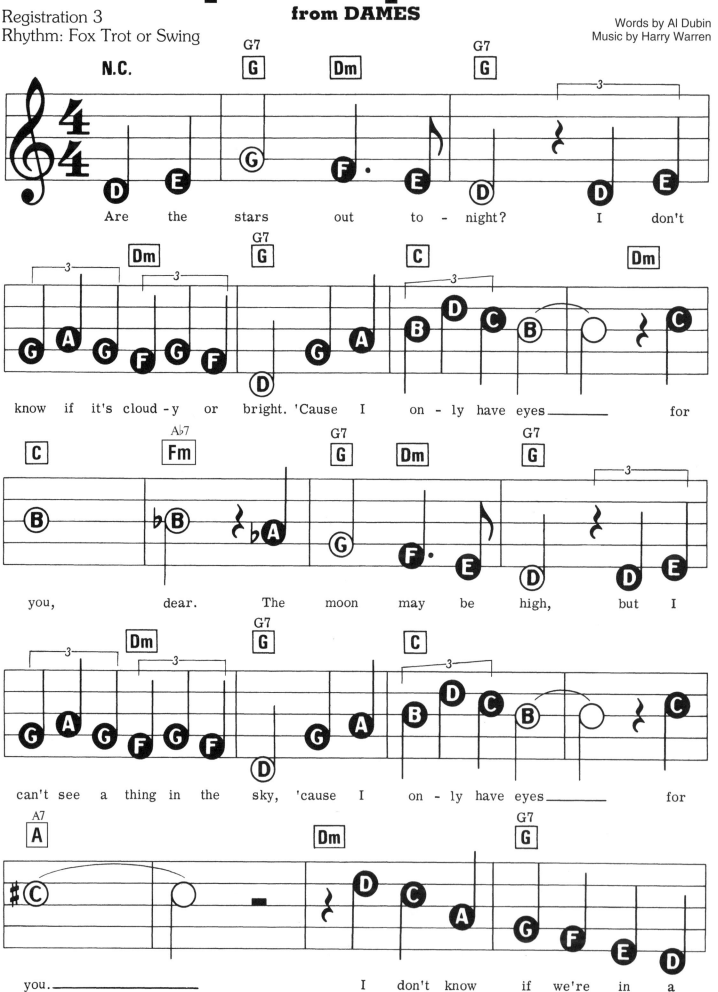

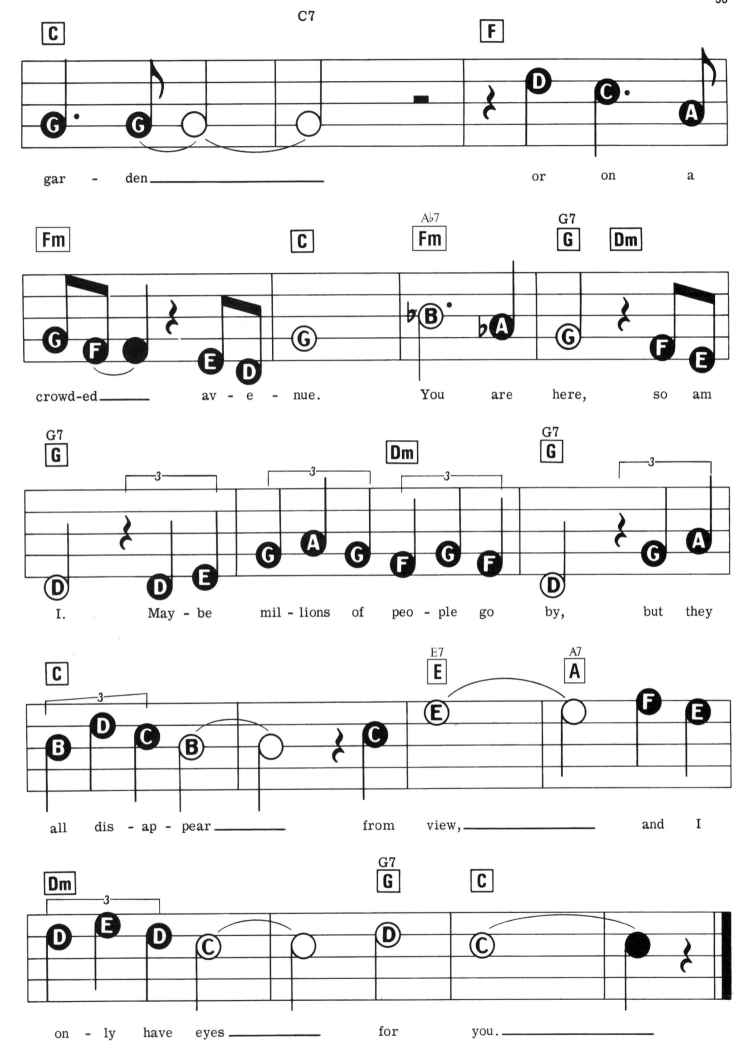

I Walk the Line

Registration 8
Rhythm: Country or Ballad

Words and Music by
John R. Cash

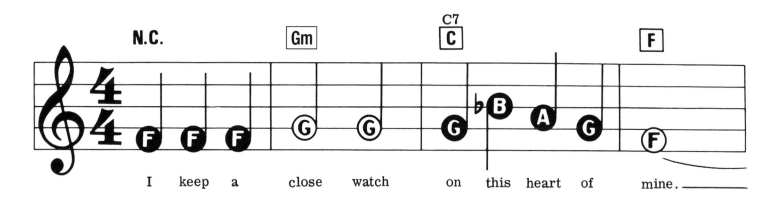

I keep a close watch on this heart of mine. _____

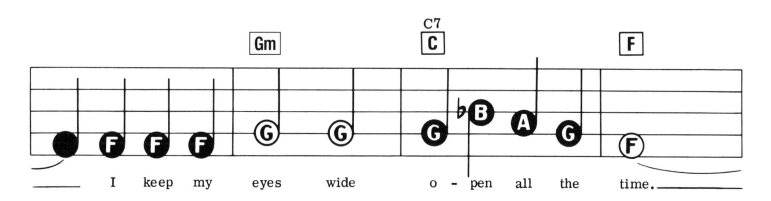

_____ I keep my eyes wide o - pen all the time. _____

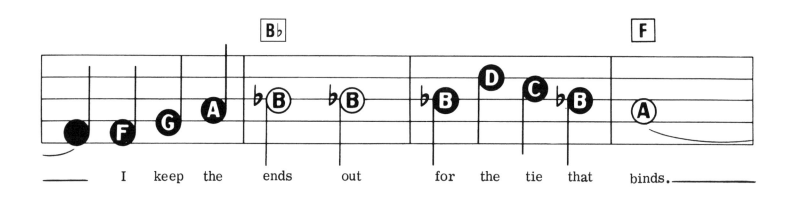

_____ I keep the ends out for the tie that binds. _____

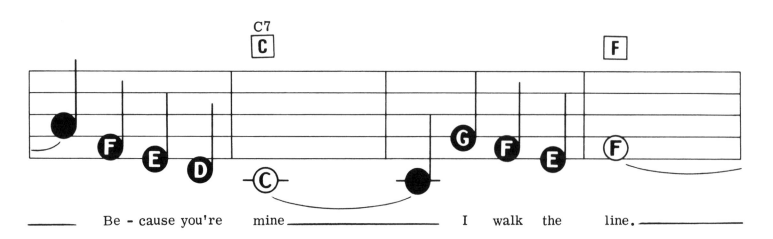

_____ Be - cause you're mine _____ I walk the line. _____

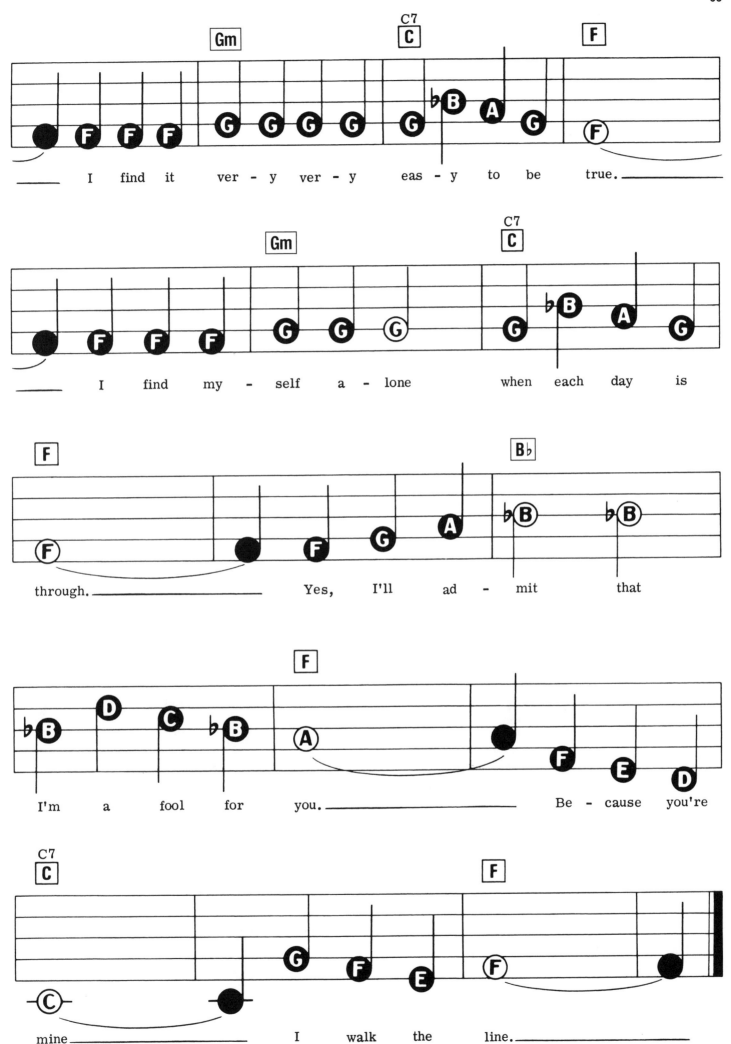

I Will Always Love You

Registration 3
Rhythm: Pops or 8-Beat

Words and Music by
Dolly Parton

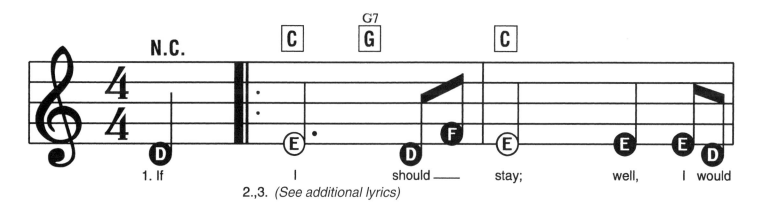

1. If I should ____ stay; well, I would

2.,3. *(See additional lyrics)*

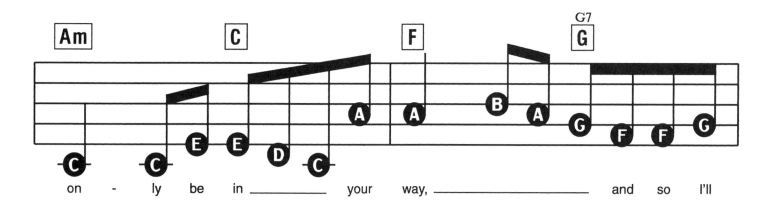

on - ly be in _____ your way, _____ and so I'll

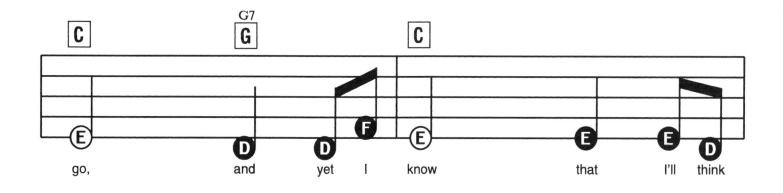

go, and yet I know that I'll think

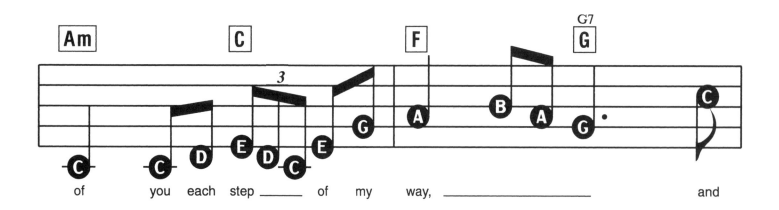

of you each step ____ of my way, _____ and

Chorus

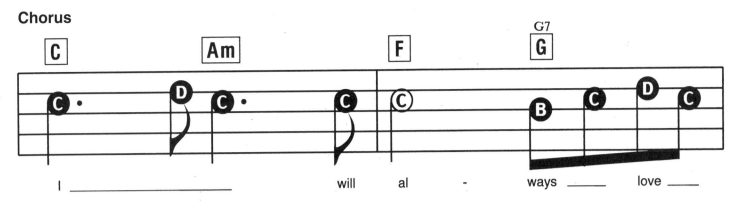

I _____ will al - ways ____ love ____

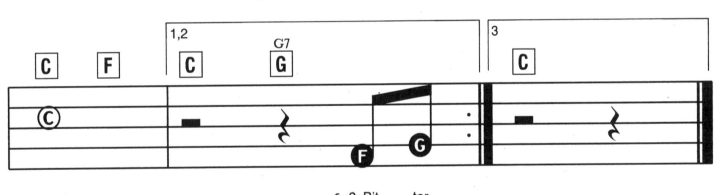

you; _____ I _____ will al - ways ____ love ____

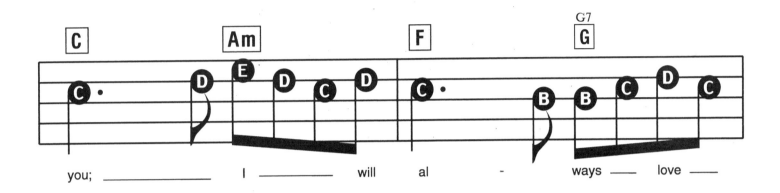

you.

{ 2. Bit - ter -
{ 3. *And* *I*

Additional Lyrics

2. Bittersweet memories, that's all I have and all I'm taking with me.
   Good-bye, oh please don't cry, 'cause we both know that I'm not what you need. But…
   Chorus

   (Spoken:)
3. *And I hope life will treat you kind, and I hope that you have all that you ever dreamed of.*
   Oh, I do wish you joy, and I wish you happiness, but above all this, I wish you love. And…
   Chorus

Layla

Registration 7
Rhythm: Rock or Heavy Metal

Words and Music by Eric Clapton
and Jim Gordon

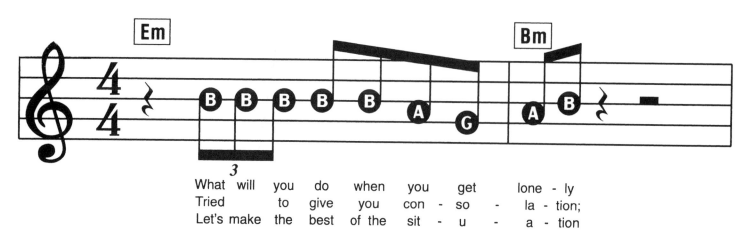

What will you do when you get lone - ly
Tried to give you con - so - la - tion;
Let's make the best of the sit - u - a - tion

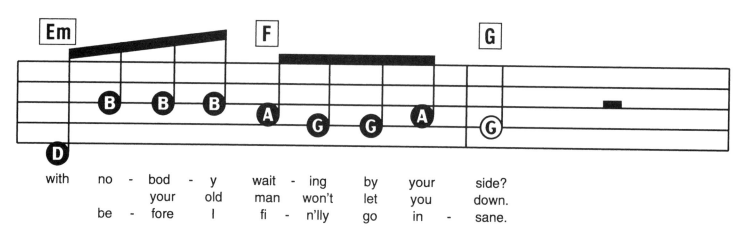

with no - bod - y wait - ing by your side?
your old man won't let you down.
be - fore I fi - n'lly go in - sane.

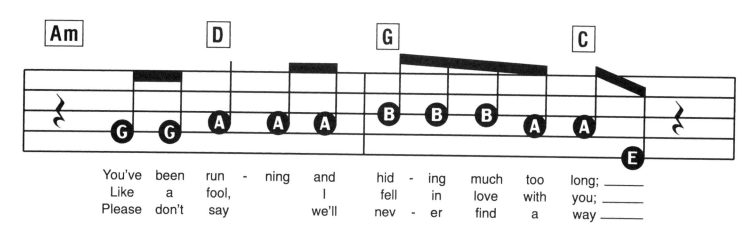

You've been run - ning and hid - ing much too long; _____
Like a fool, I fell in love too with you; _____
Please don't say we'll nev - er find a way _____

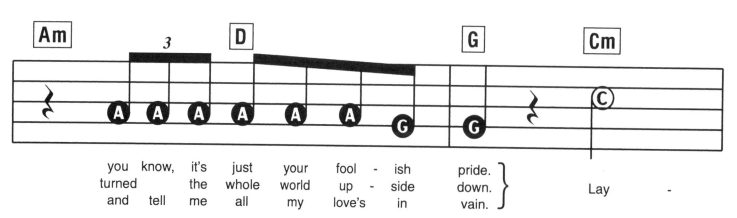

you know, it's just your fool - ish pride.
turned the whole world up - side down.   } Lay -
and tell me all my love's in vain.

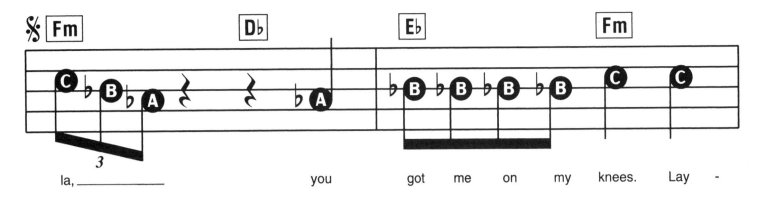

la, _____ you got me on my knees. Lay -

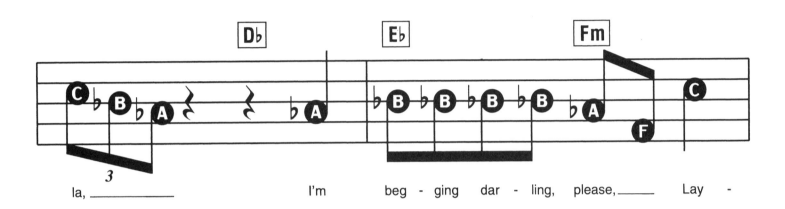

la, _____ I'm beg - ging dar - ling, please, _____ Lay -

To Coda ⊕

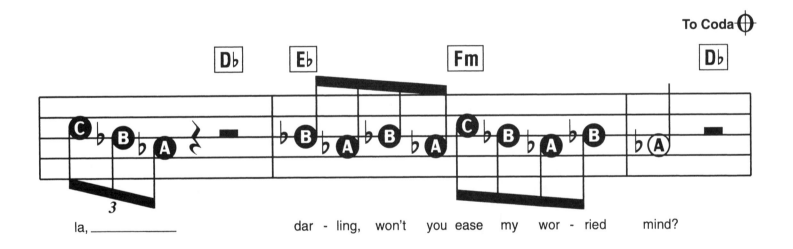

la, _____ dar - ling, won't you ease my wor - ried mind?

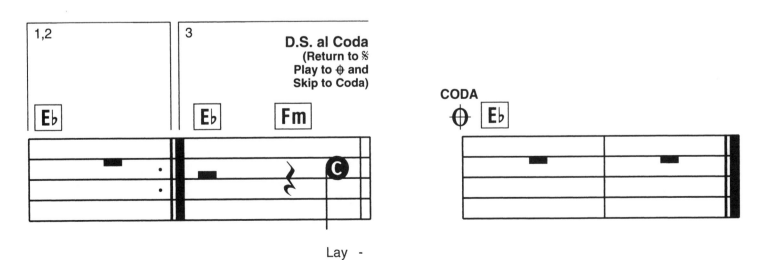

Lay -

D.S. al Coda
(Return to %
Play to ⊕ and
Skip to Coda)

CODA
⊕

Let It Go

Registration 8
Rhythm: Rock or Dance

Music and Lyrics by Kristen Anderson-Lopez
and Robert Lopez

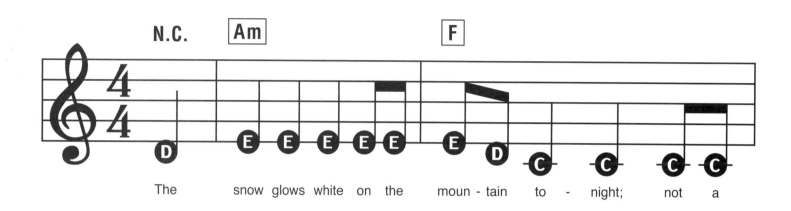

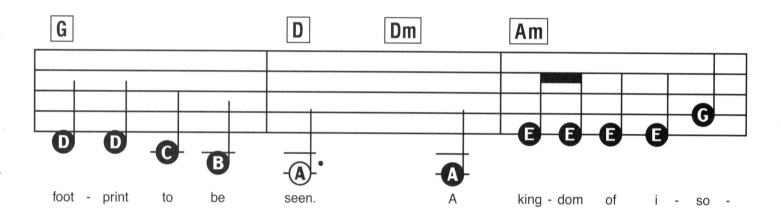

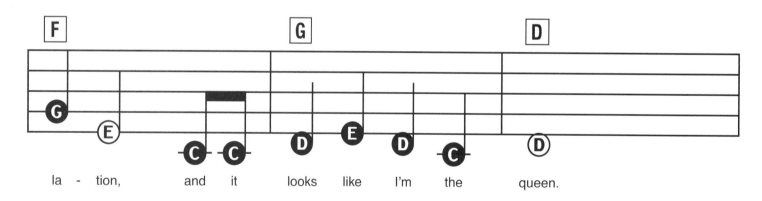

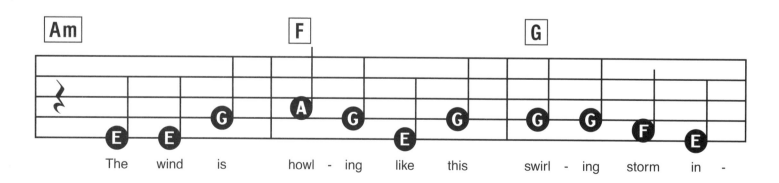

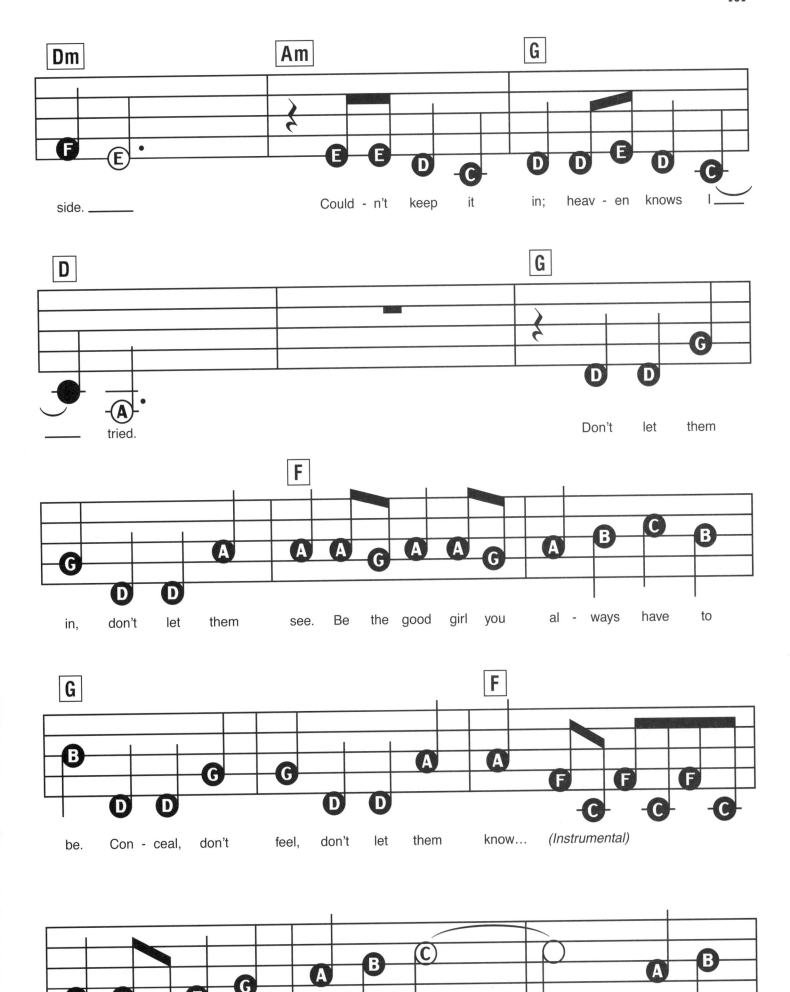

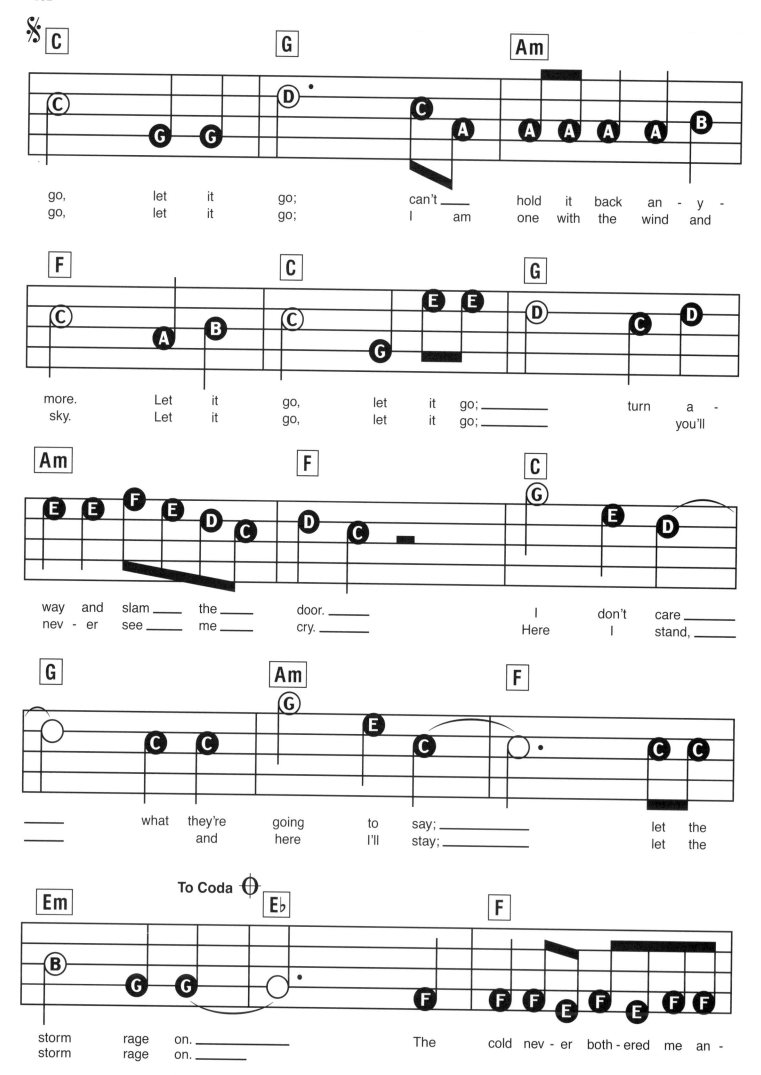

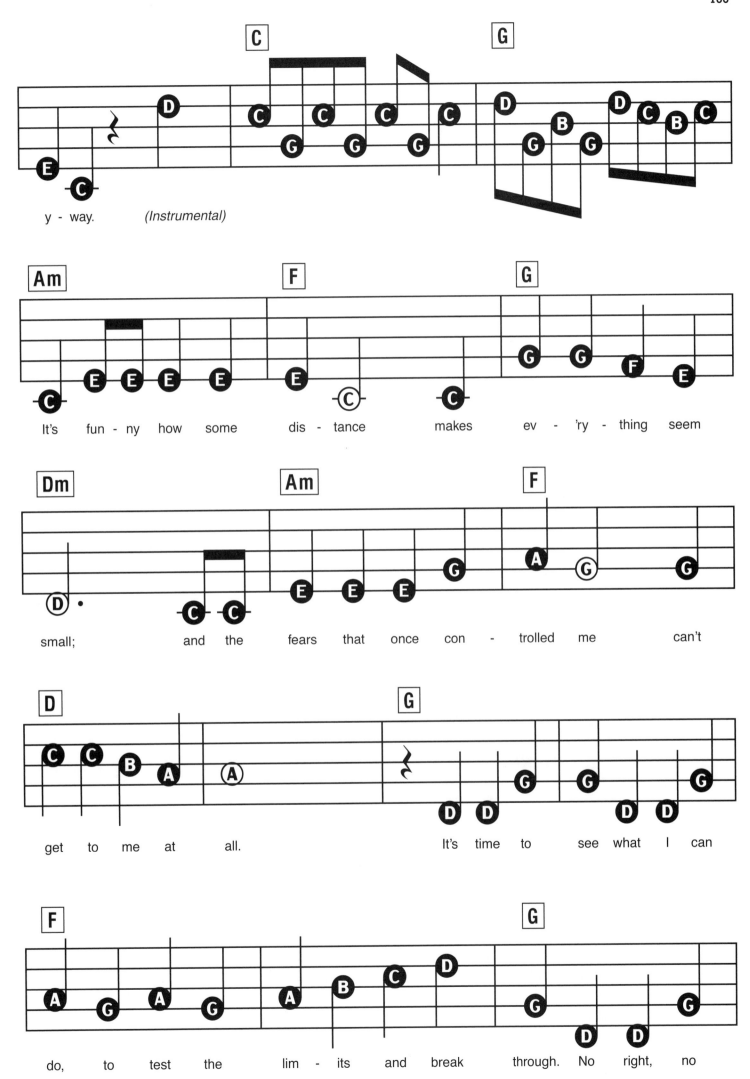

D.S. al Coda
(Return to %
Play to ⊕ and
Skip to Coda)

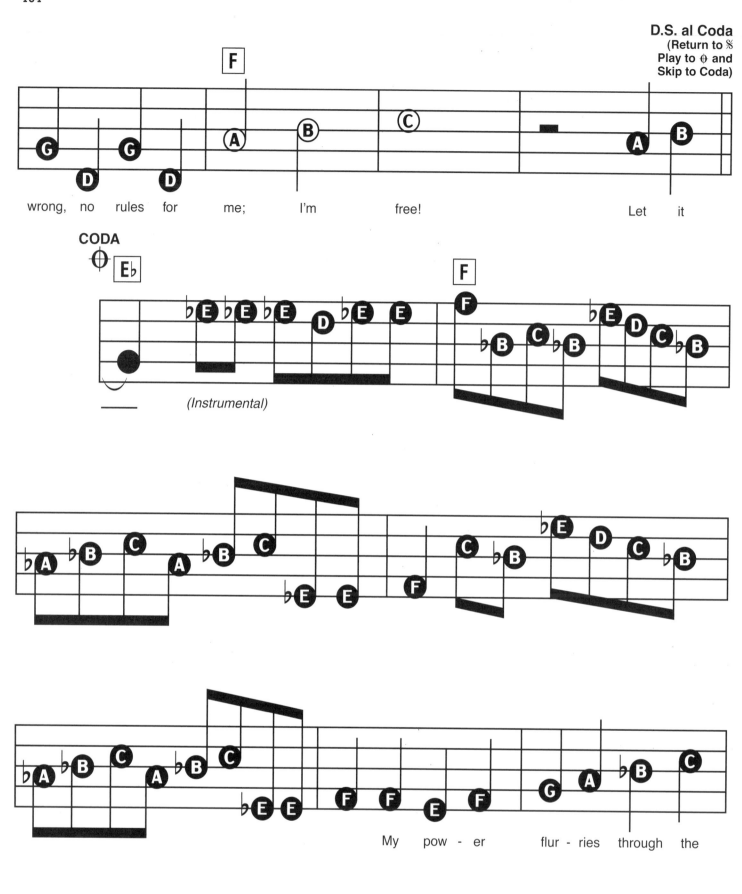

wrong, no rules for me; I'm free! Let it

CODA

(Instrumental)

My pow - er flur - ries through the

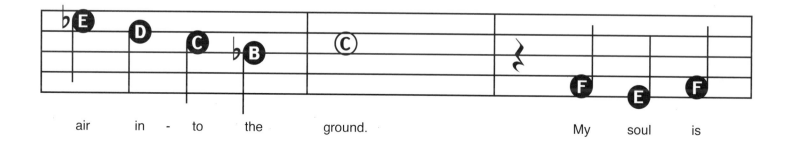

air in - to the ground. My soul is

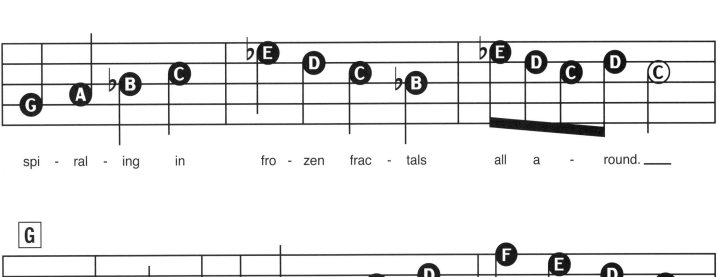

spi - ral - ing in fro - zen frac - tals all a - round. ___

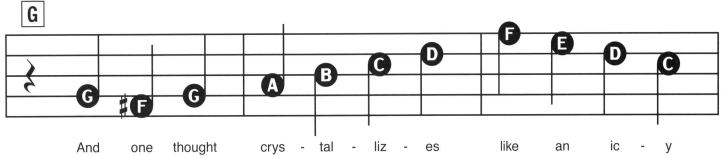

And one thought crys - tal - liz - es like an ic - y

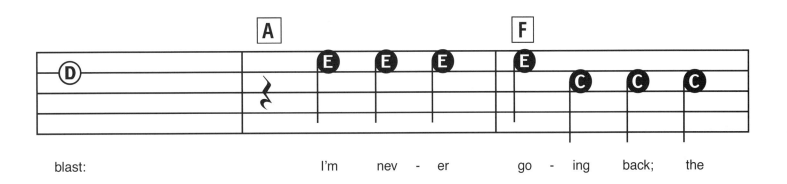

blast: I'm nev - er go - ing back; the

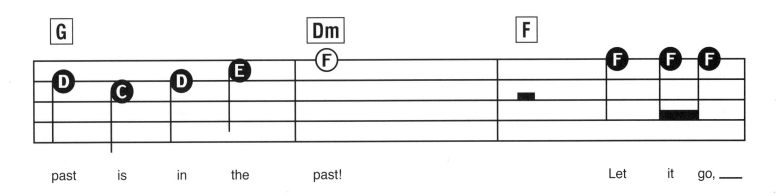

past is in the past! Let it go, ___

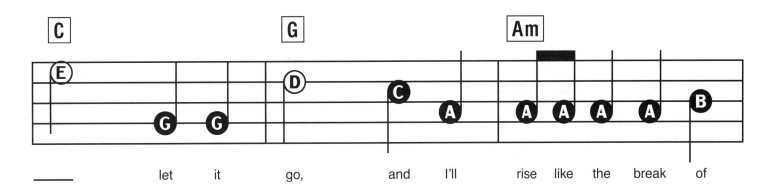

___ let it go, and I'll rise like the break of

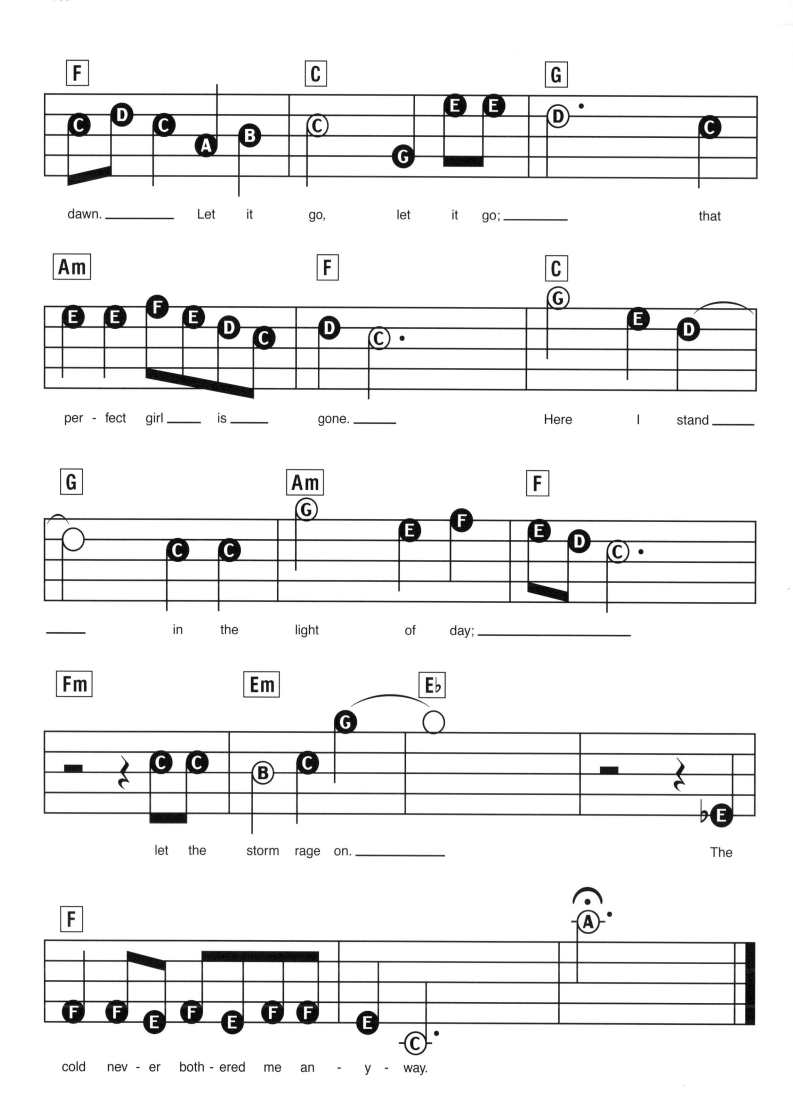

Mrs. Robinson
from THE GRADUATE

Registration 5
Rhythm: Swing

Words and Music by
Paul Simon

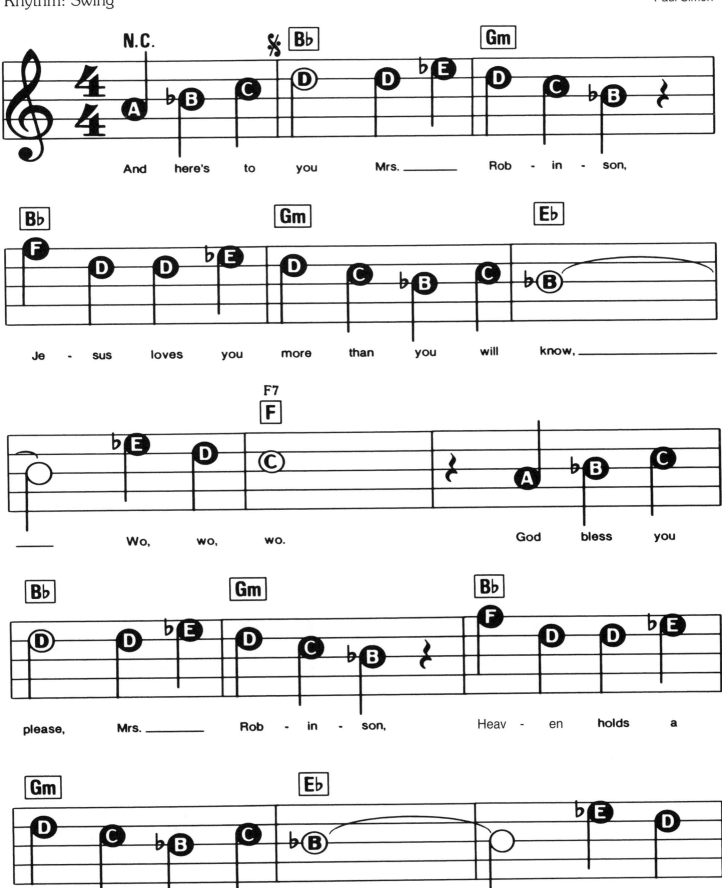

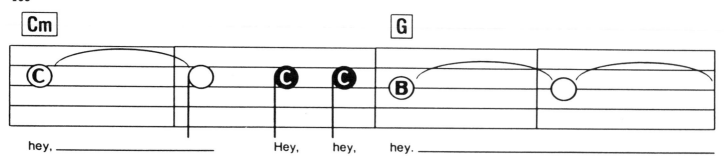

hey, _____ Hey, hey, hey. _____

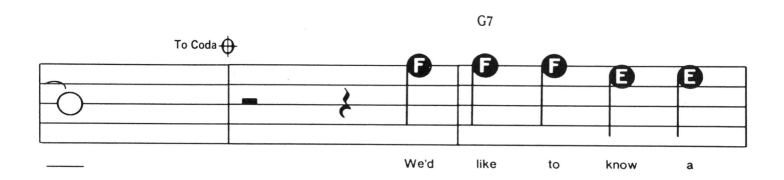

_____ We'd like to know a

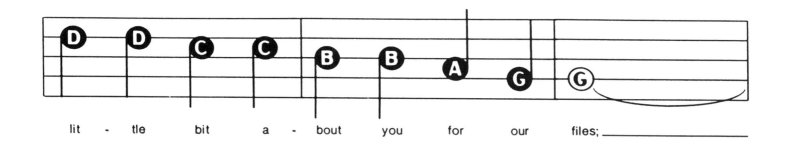

lit - tle bit a - bout you for our files; _____

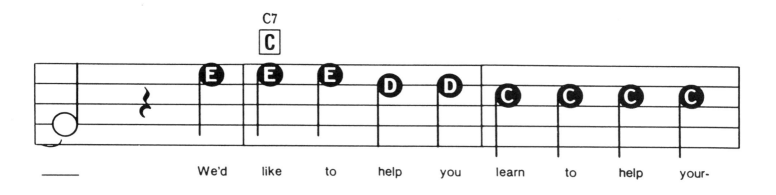

_____ We'd like to help you learn to help your-

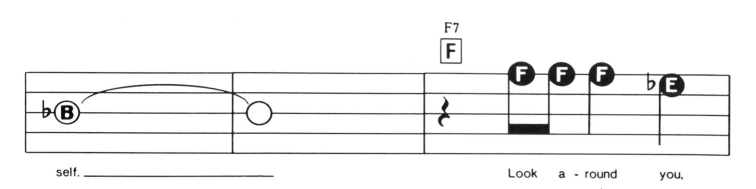

self. _____ Look a - round you,

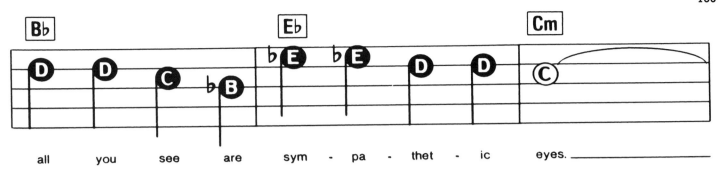

all you see are sym - pa - thet - ic eyes. _____

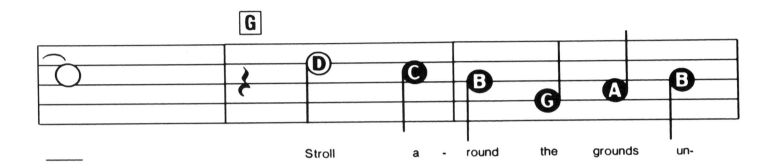

_____ Stroll a - round the grounds un-

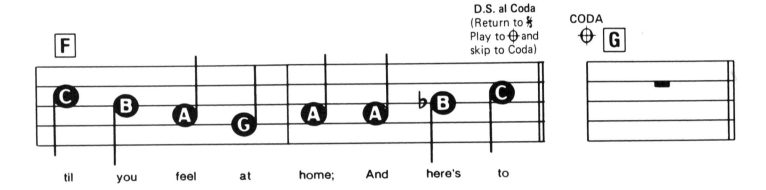

D.S. al Coda
(Return to 𝄋
Play to ⊕ and
skip to Coda)

CODA
⊕ G

til you feel at home; And here's to

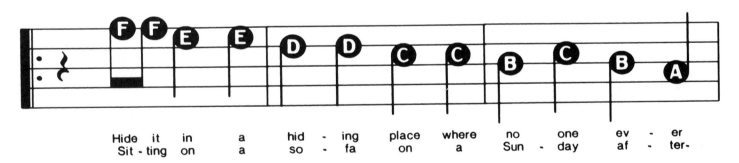

Hide it in a hid - ing place where no one ev - er
Sit - ting on a so - fa place on a Sun - day af - ter-

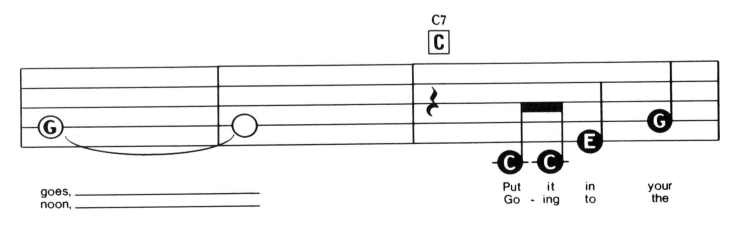

goes, _____
noon, _____

Put it in your
Go - ing to the

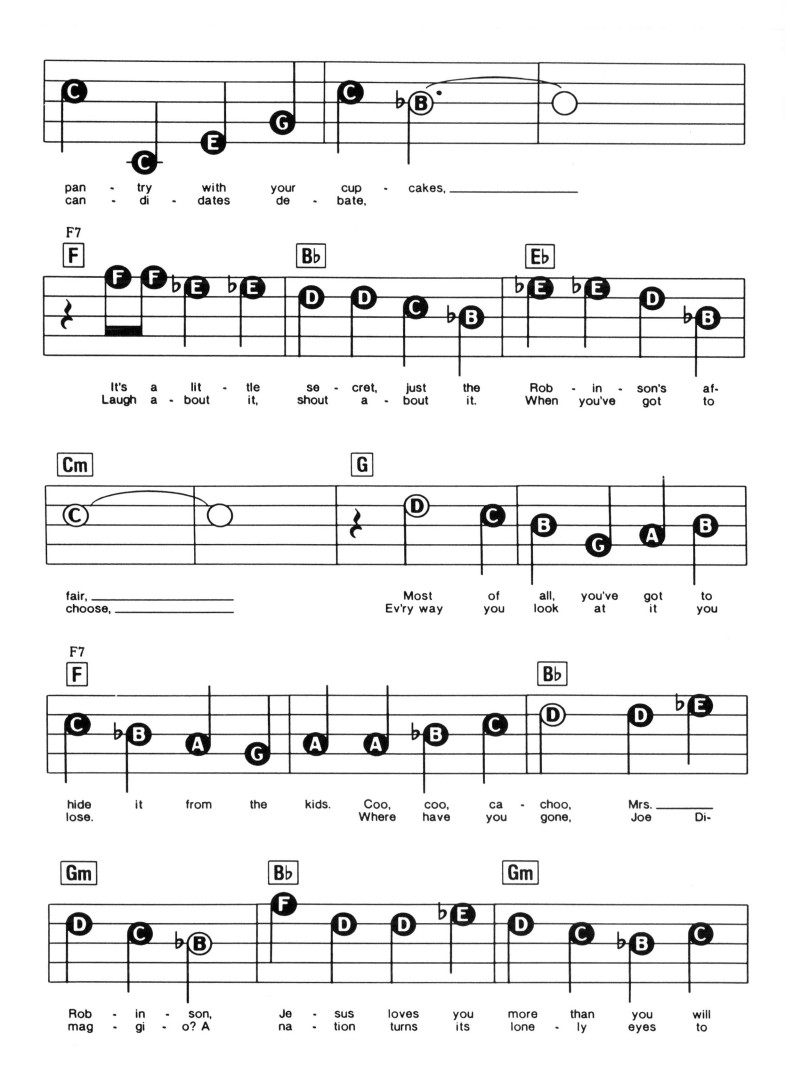

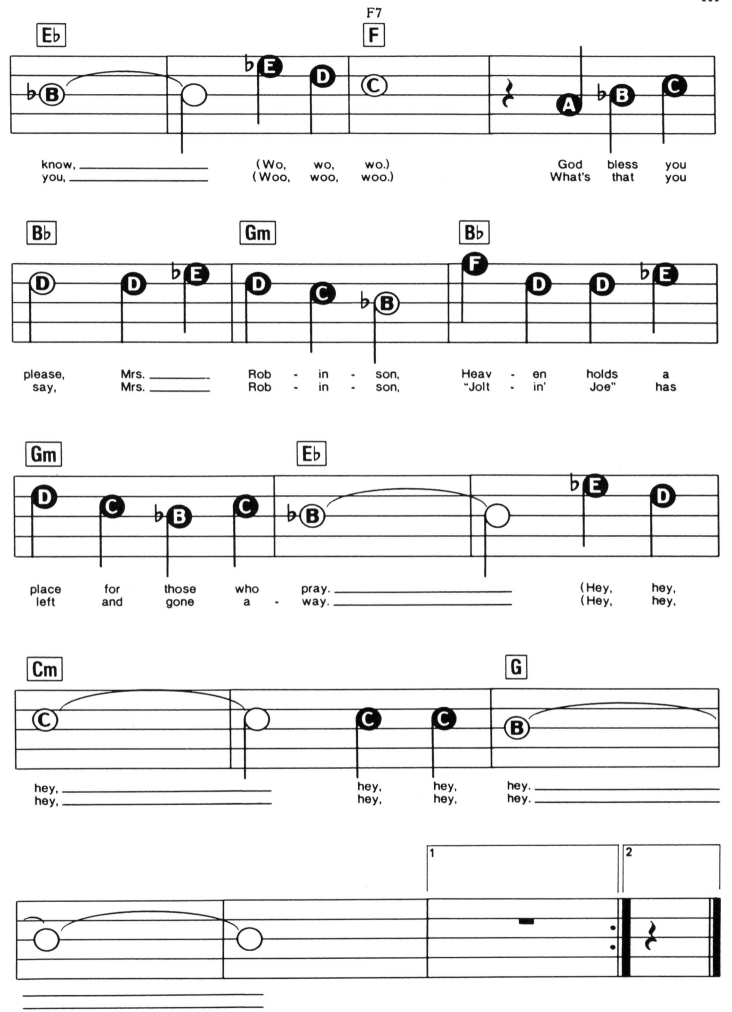

Mr. Bojangles

Registration 3
Rhythm: Waltz

Words and Music by
Jerry Jeff Walker

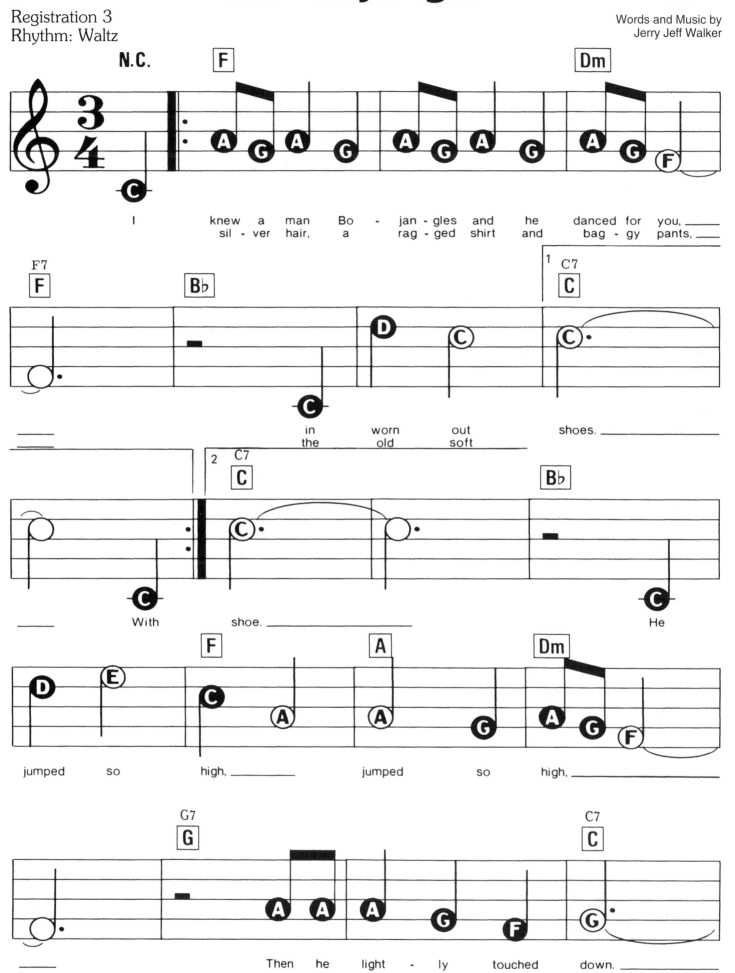

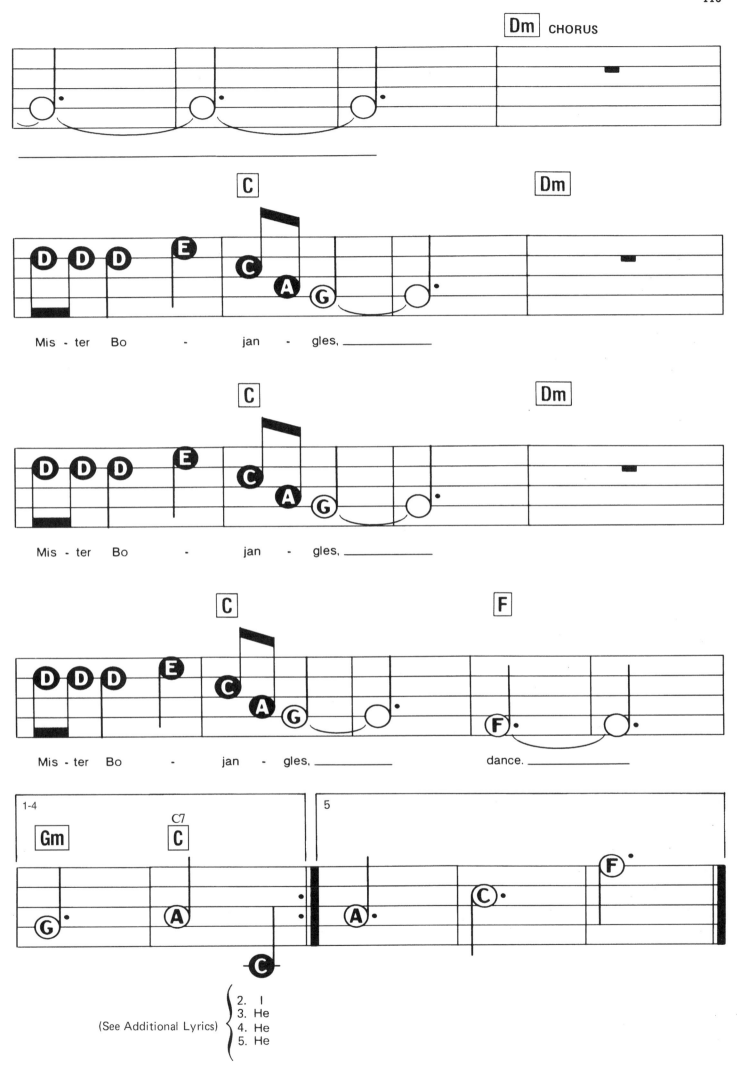

Mis - ter Bo - jan - gles, _____

Mis - ter Bo - jan - gles, _____

Mis - ter Bo - jan - gles, _____ dance. _____

(See Additional Lyrics)
2. I
3. He
4. He
5. He

Additional Lyrics

Verse 2   I met him in a cell in New Orleans
           I was down and out.
           He looked at me to be the eyes of age
           As he spoke right out.
           He talked of life, talked of life,
           He laughed slapped his leg a step.
           (Chorus)

Verse 3   He said his name, Bojangles,
           Then he danced a lick across the cell.
           He grabbed his pants a better stance
           Oh, he jumped up high,
           He clicked his heels.
           He let go a laugh, let go a laugh,
           Shook back his clothes all around
           (Chorus)

Verse 4   He danced for those at minstrel shows
           And county fairs throughout the South.
           He spoke with tears of fifteen years
           How his dog and he traveled about.
           His dog up and died, he up and died,
           After twenty years he still grieved.
           (Chorus)

Verse 5   He said, "I dance now at every chance
           In honky tonks for drinks and tips.
           But most of the time I spend behind these county bars."
           He said, "I drinks a bit."
           He shook his head
           And as he shook his head, I heard someone ask please
           (Chorus)

My Valentine

Registration 4
Rhythm: Ballad

Words and Music by
Paul McCartney

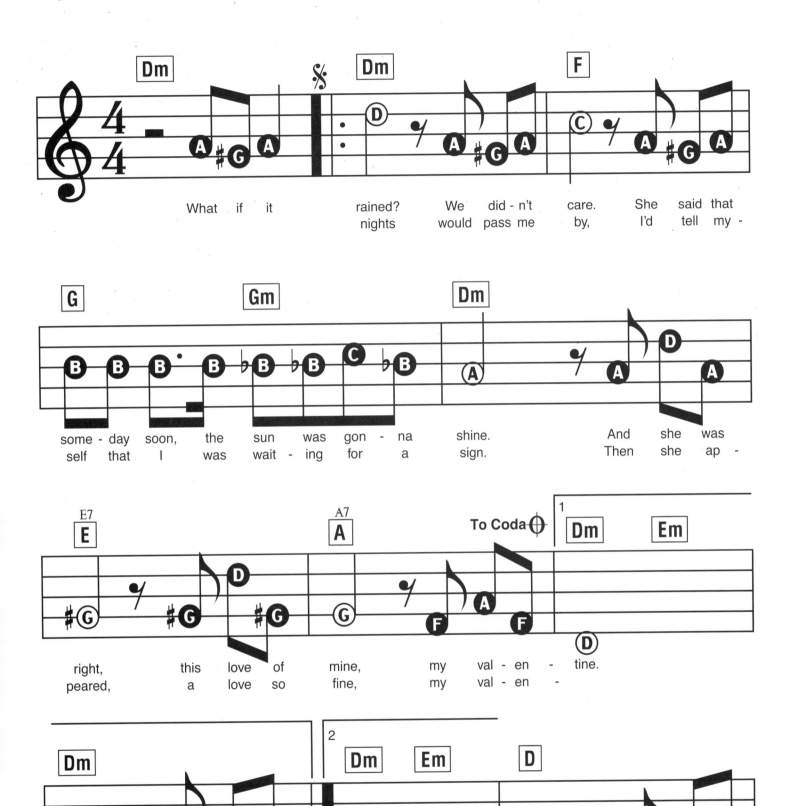

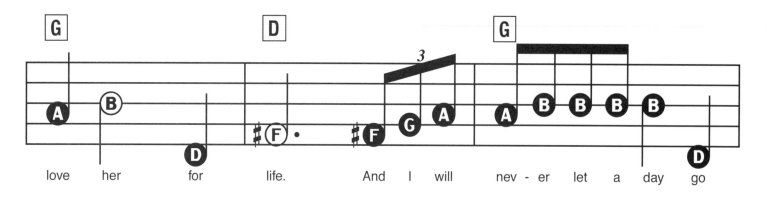

love her for life. And I will nev - er let a day go

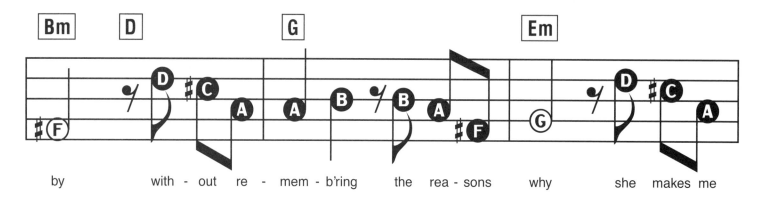

by with - out re - mem - b'ring the rea - sons why she makes me

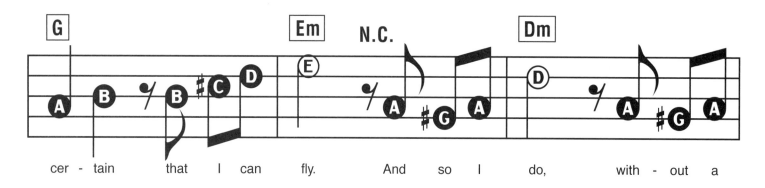

cer - tain that I can fly. And so I do, with - out a

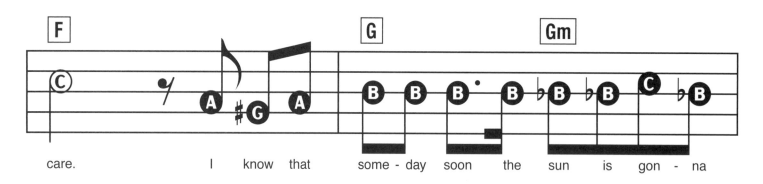

care. I know that some - day soon the sun is gon - na

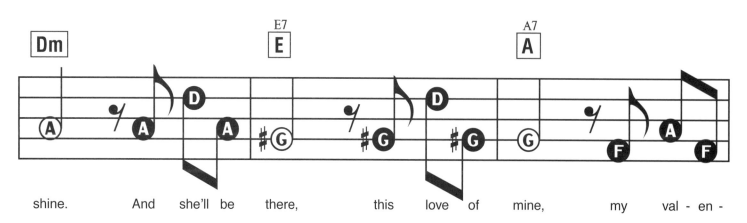

shine. And she'll be there, this love of mine, my val - en -

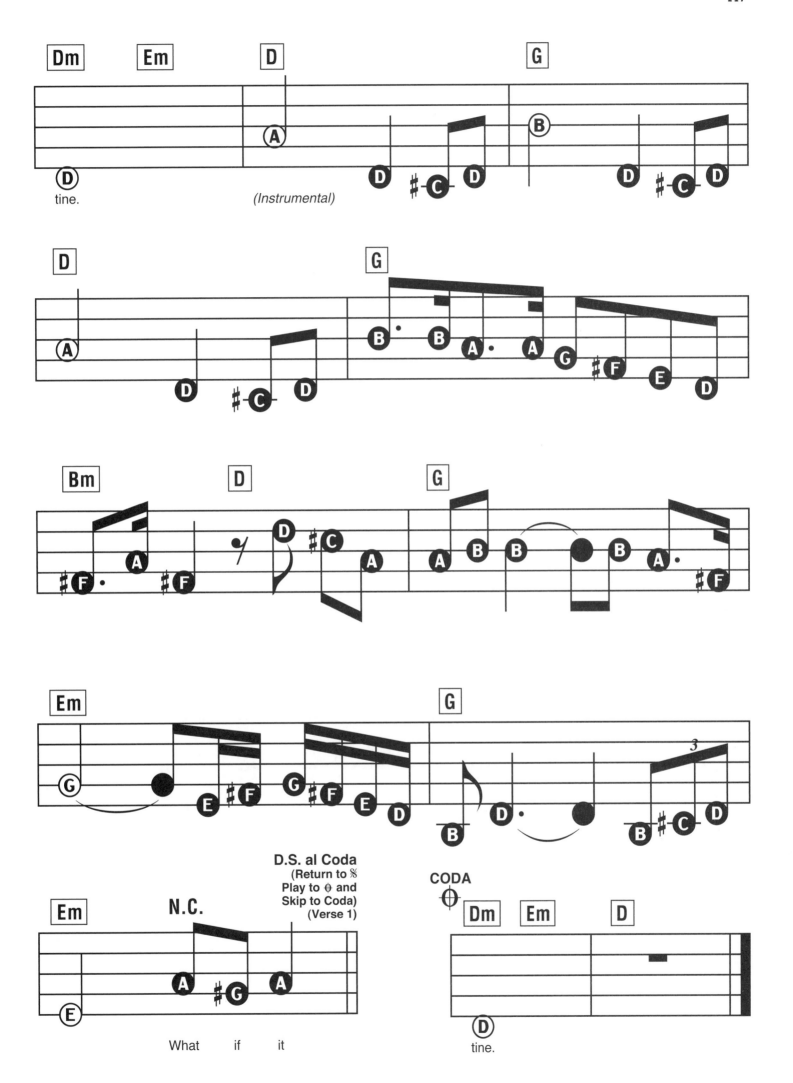

My Favorite Things
from THE SOUND OF MUSIC

Registration 1
Rhythm: Waltz

Lyrics by Oscar Hammerstein II
Music by Richard Rodgers

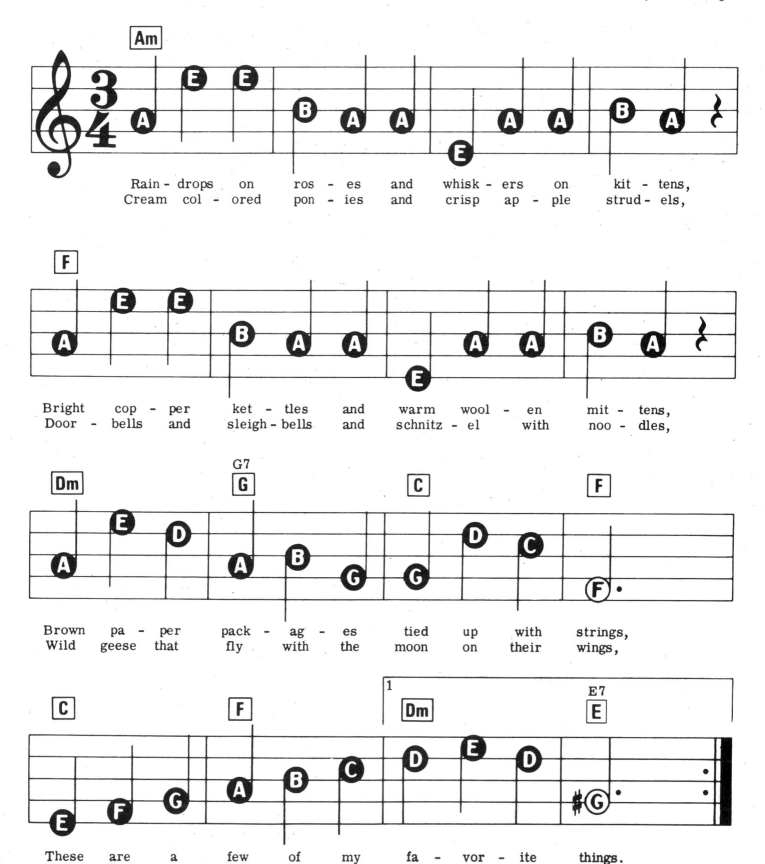

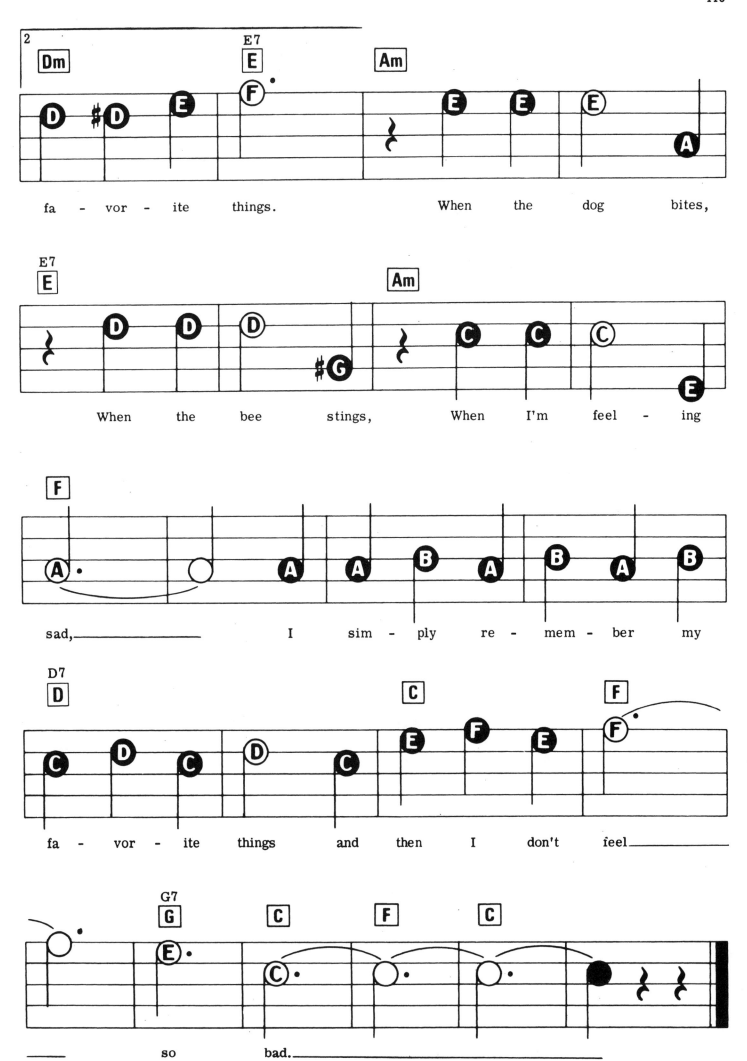

Over the Rainbow
from THE WIZARD OF OZ

Registration 5
Rhythm: Ballad

Music by Harold Arlen
Lyric by E.Y. "Yip" Harburg

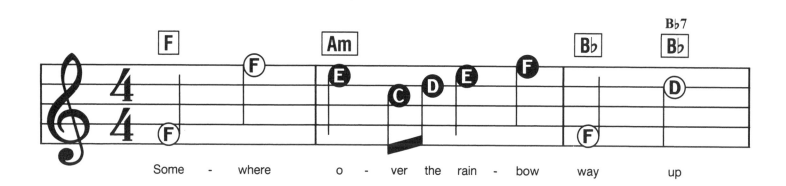

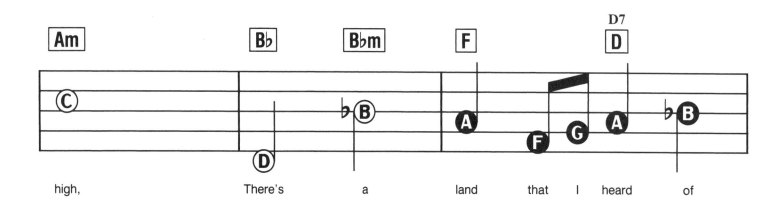

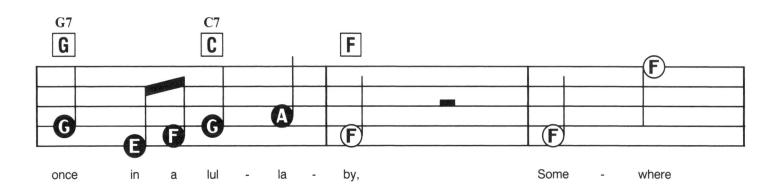

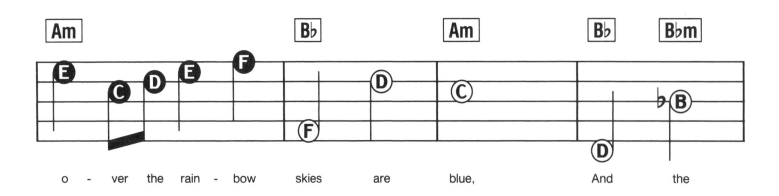

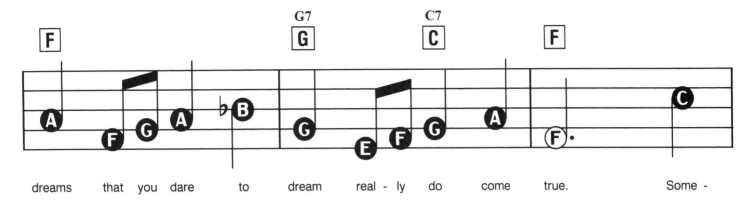

dreams that you dare to dream real - ly do come true. Some -

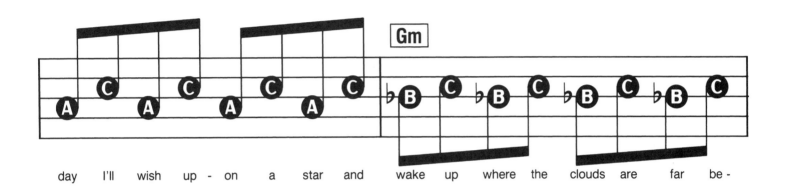

day I'll wish up - on a star and wake up where the clouds are far be -

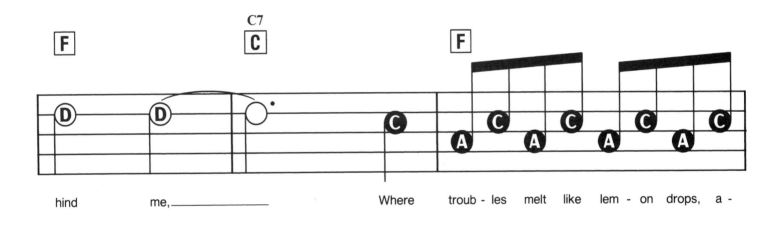

hind me,_____ Where troub - les melt like lem - on drops, a -

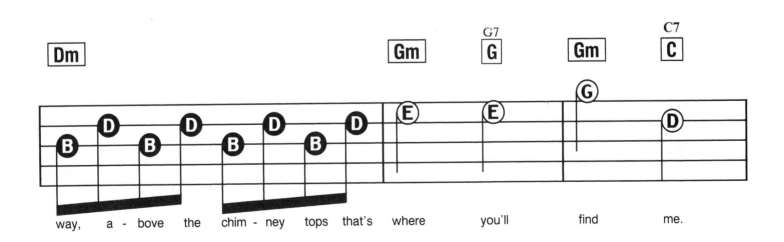

way, a - bove the chim - ney tops that's where you'll find me.

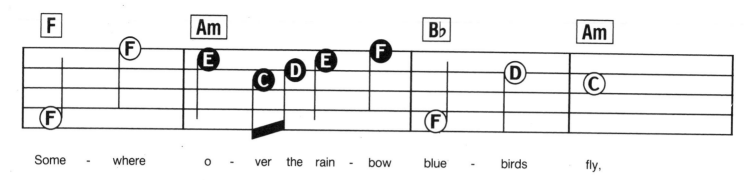

Some - where o - ver the rain - bow blue - birds fly,

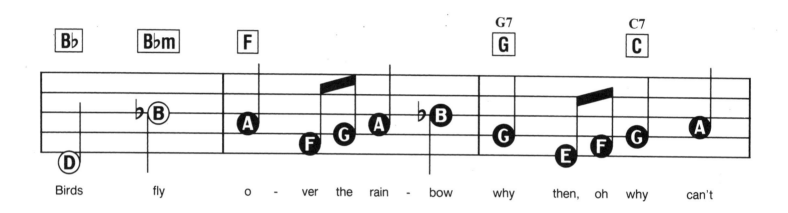

Birds fly o - ver the rain - bow why then, oh why can't

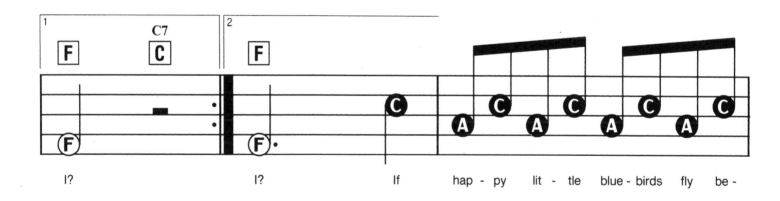

I? I? If hap - py lit - tle blue - birds fly be -

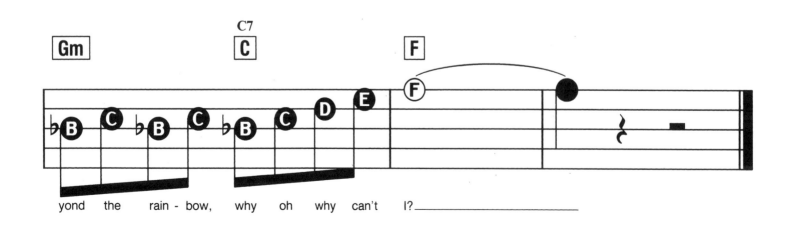

yond the rain - bow, why oh why can't I?

The Rainbow Connection
from THE MUPPET MOVIE

Registration 4
Rhythm: Waltz

Words and Music by Paul Williams
and Kenneth L. Ascher

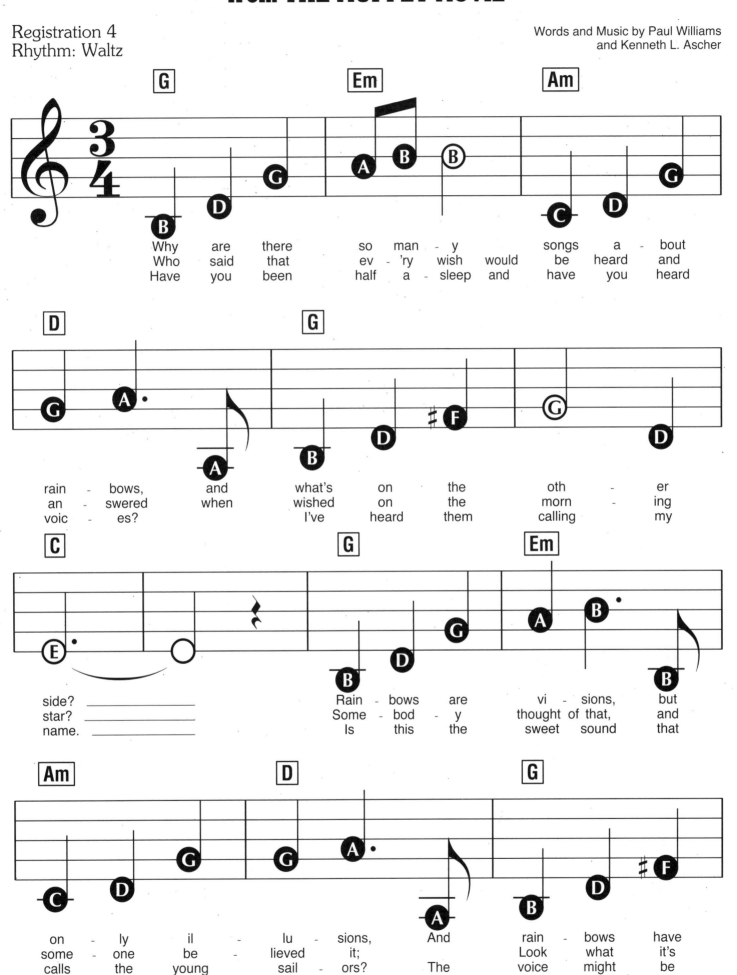

124

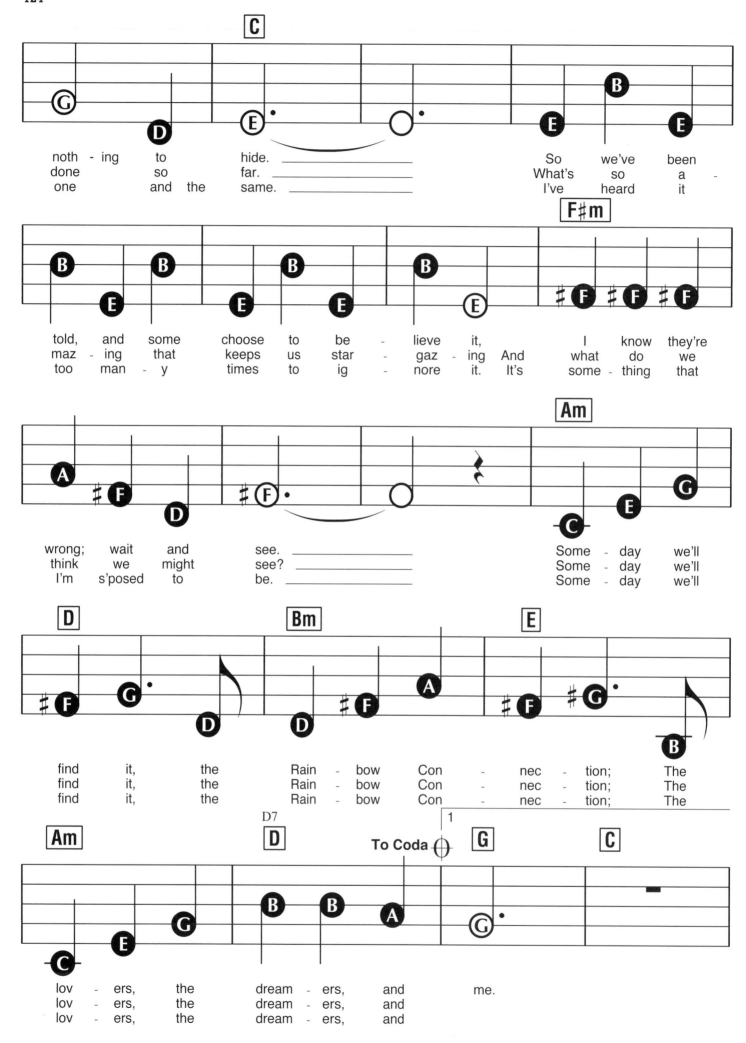

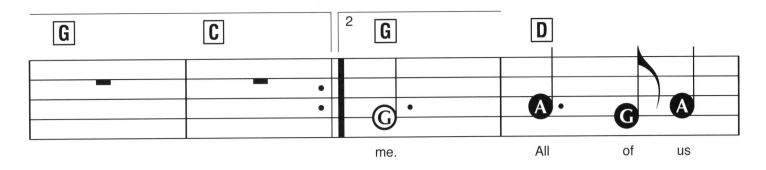

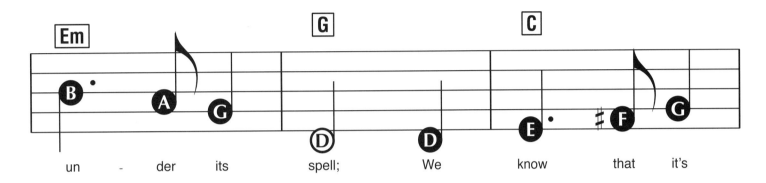

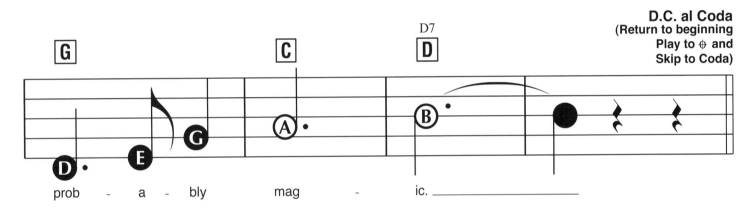

D7

D.C. al Coda
(Return to beginning
Play to ⊕ and
Skip to Coda)

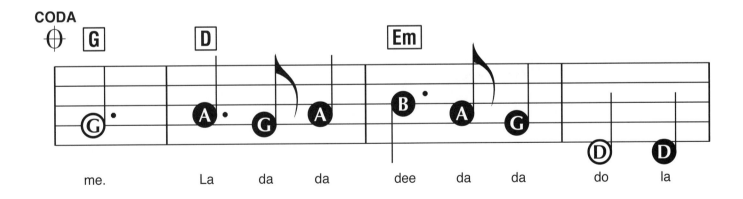

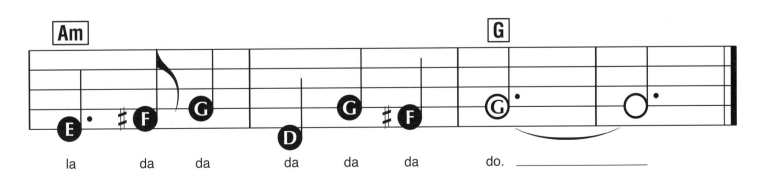

Respect

Registration 8
Rhythm: Rock

Words and Music by
Otis Redding

What you want ba - by I got.
I ain't gonna do you wrong while _____ you gone.

What you need you know I got it.
I ain't gonna do you need wrong 'Cause I don't wan - na.

All I'm ask - in' is for a lit - tle re -

spect, when you come home. Ba - by, when you come

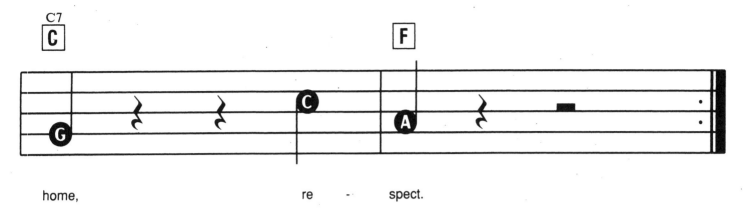

home, re - spect.

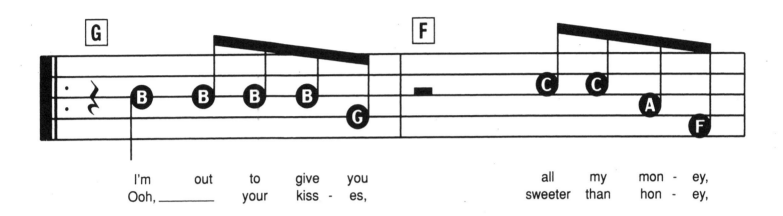

I'm out to give you all my mon - ey,
Ooh, _____ your kiss - es, sweeter than hon - ey,

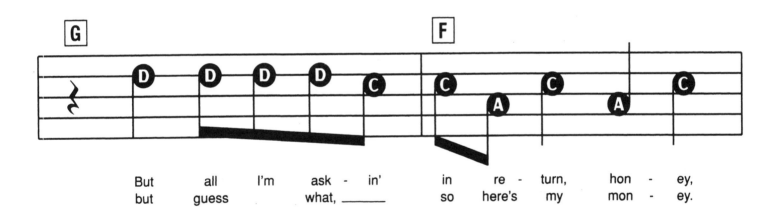

But all I'm ask - in' in re - turn, hon - ey,
but guess what, _____ so here's my mon - ey.

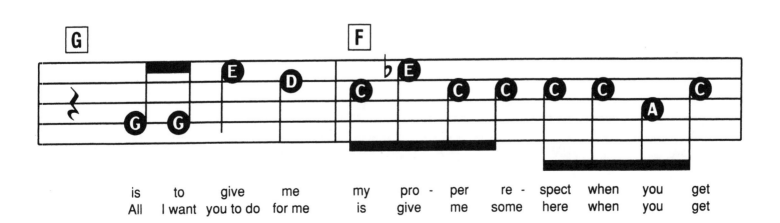

is to give me my pro - per re - spect when you get
All I want you to do for me is give me some here when you get

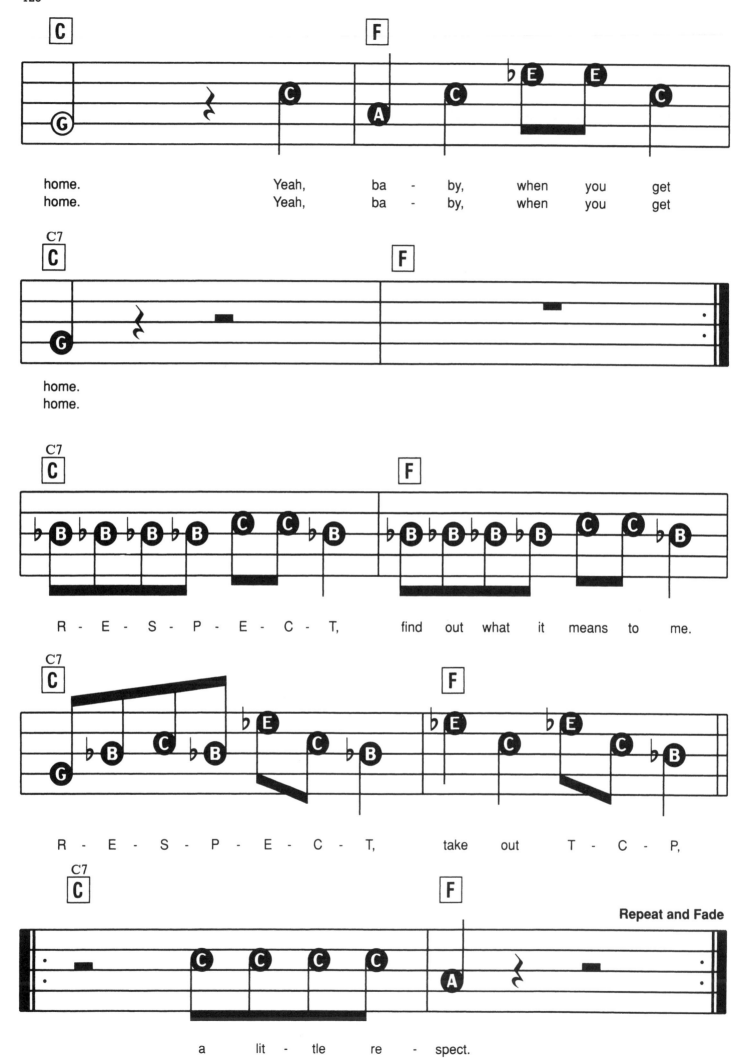

Rock with You

Registration 2
Rhythm: Rock

Words and Music by
Rod Temperton

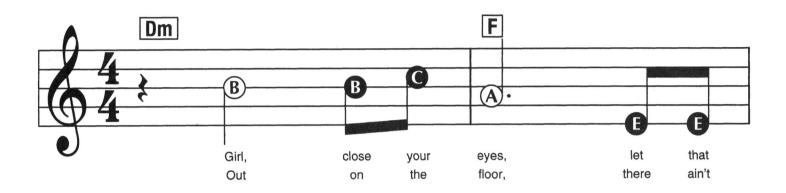

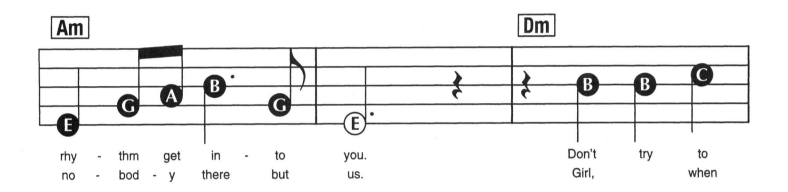

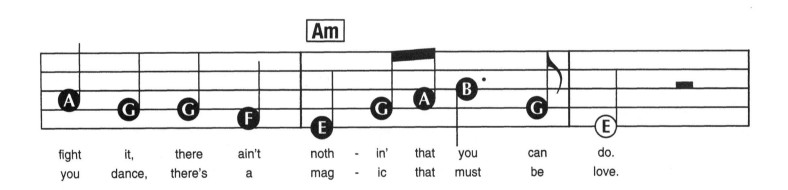

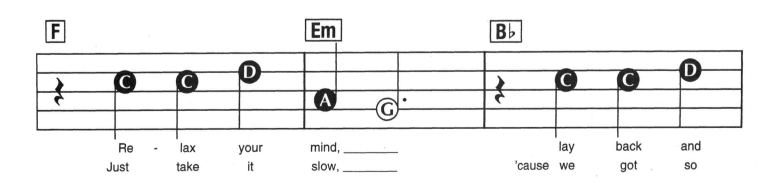

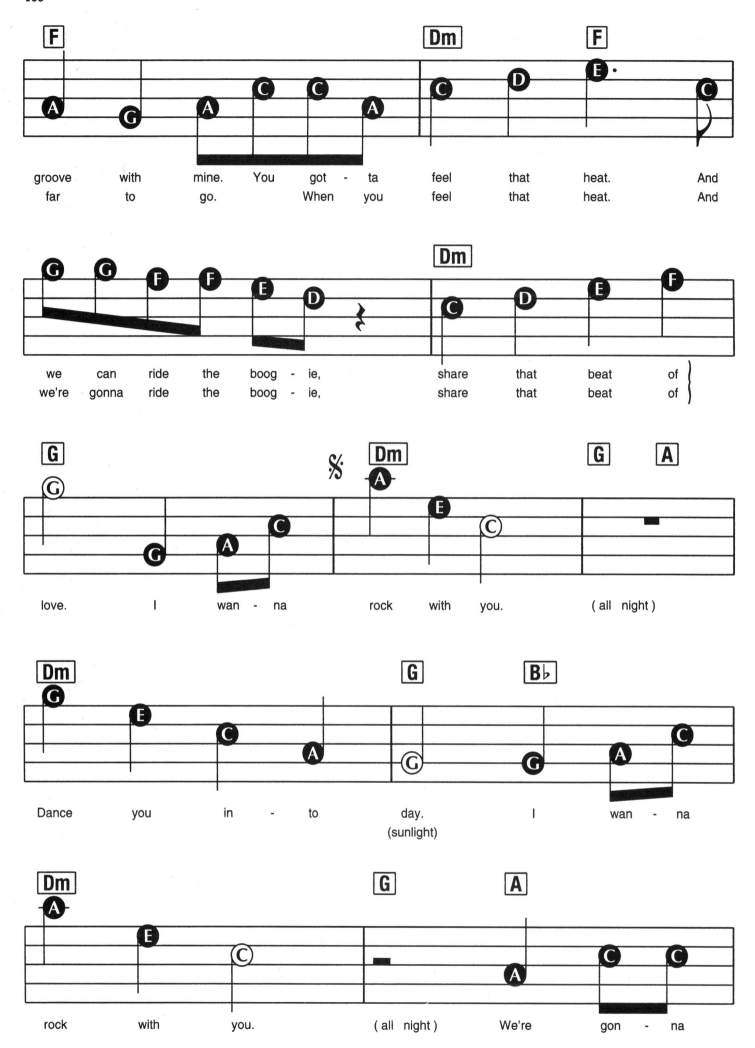

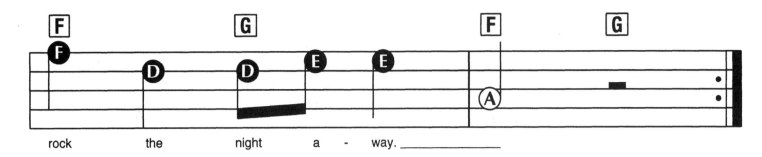

rock   the   night   a - way. _____

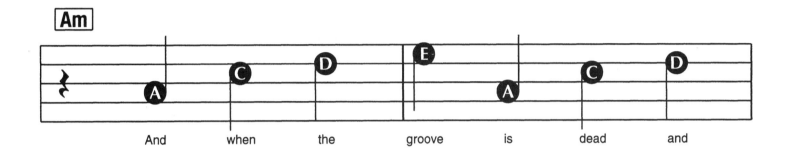

And   when   the   groove   is   dead   and

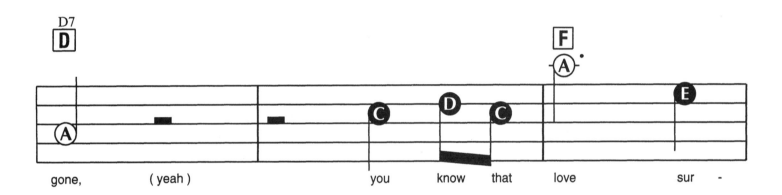

gone,   (yeah)   you   know   that   love   sur -

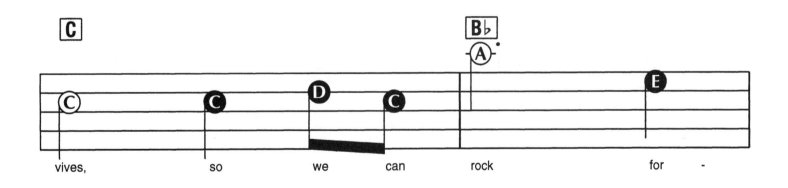

vives,   so   we   can   rock   for -

D.S. and Fade
(Return to %
and Fade)

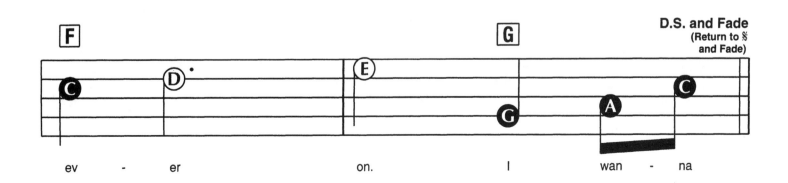

ev - er   on.   I   wan - na

Stairway to Heaven

Registration 4
Rhythm: Slow Rock or Ballad

Words and Music by Jimmy Page
and Robert Plant

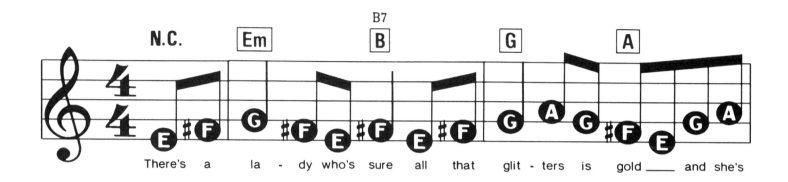

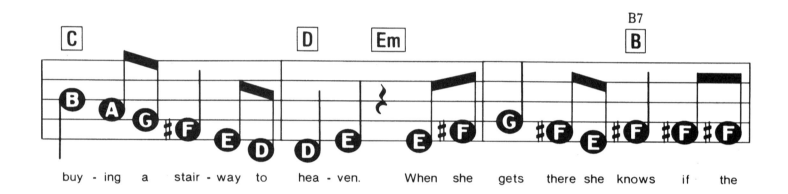

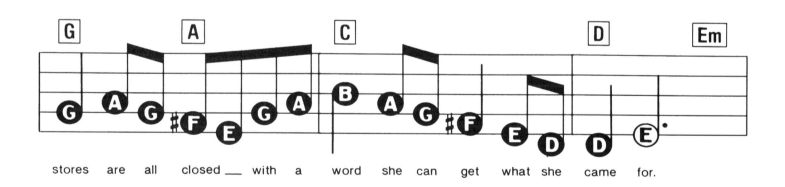

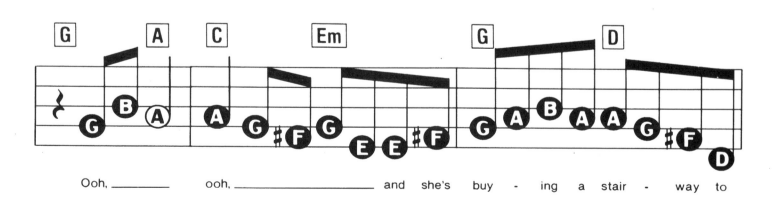

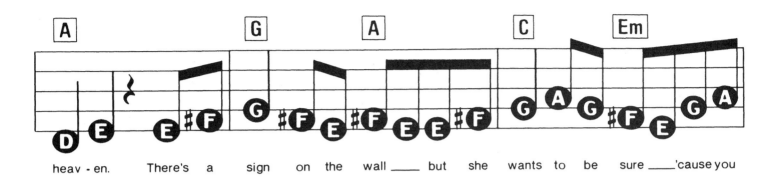

heav - en. There's a sign on the wall ___ but she wants to be sure ___'cause you

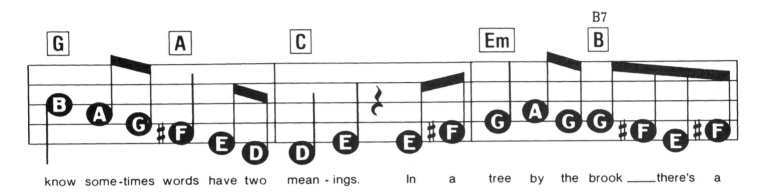

know some-times words have two mean - ings. In a tree by the brook ___ there's a

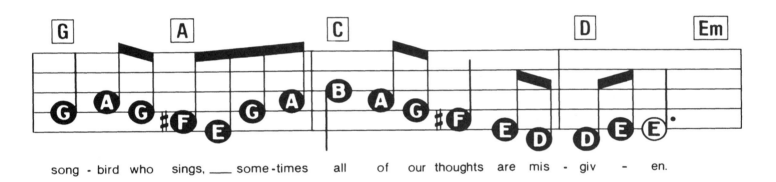

song - bird who sings, ___ some-times all of our thoughts are mis - giv – en.

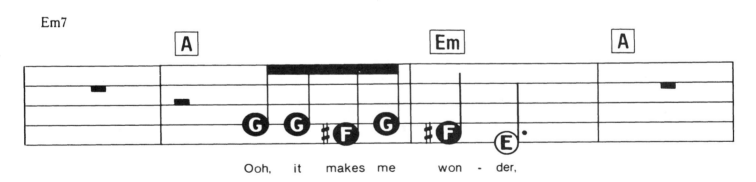

Ooh, it makes me won - der,

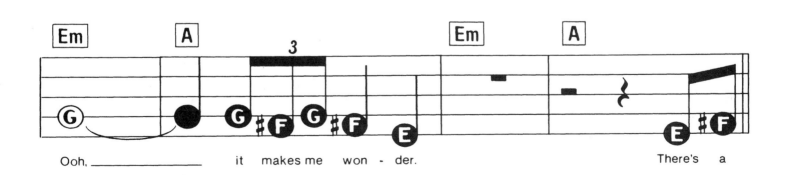

Ooh, ___ it makes me won - der. There's a

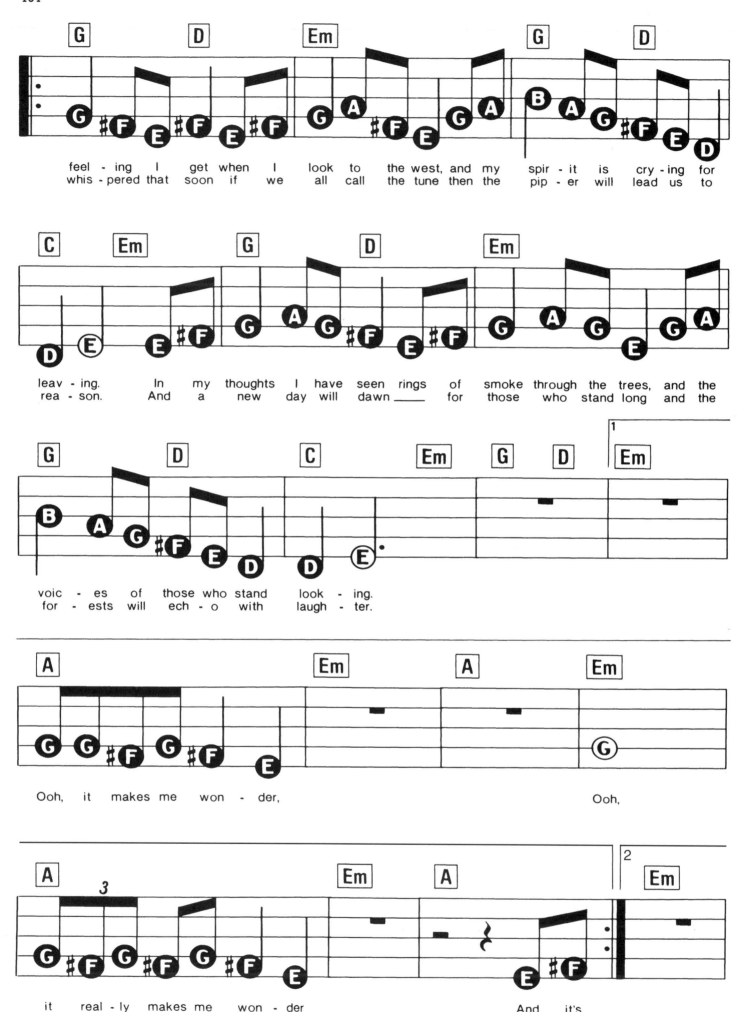

135

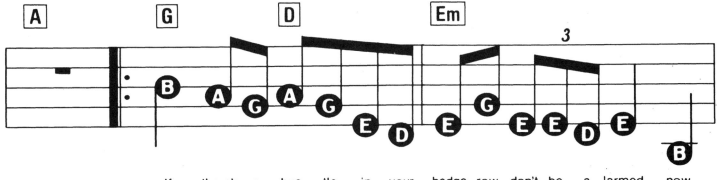

If there's a bus-tle in your hedge-row don't be a-larmed now,
Your head is hum-ming and it won't go in case you don't know,

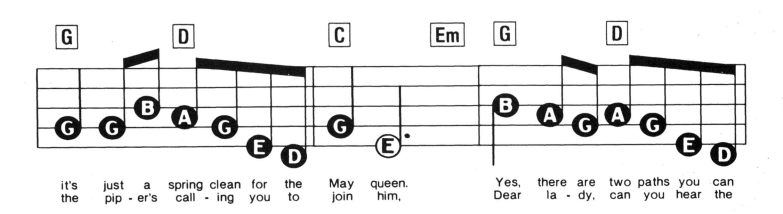

it's just a spring clean for the May queen.
the pip-er's call-ing you to join him,

Yes, there are two paths you can
Dear la-dy, can you hear the

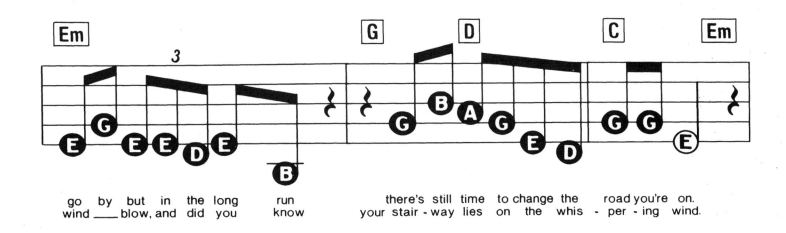

go by but in the long run
wind ___ blow, and did you know

there's still time to change the road you're on.
your stair-way lies on the whis-per-ing wind.

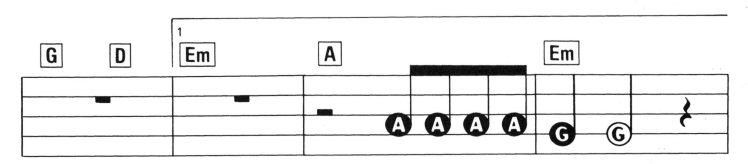

And it makes me won-der.

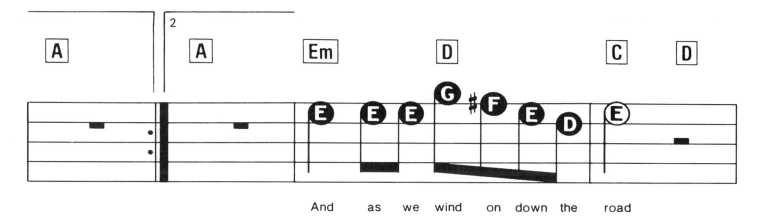

And as we wind on down the road

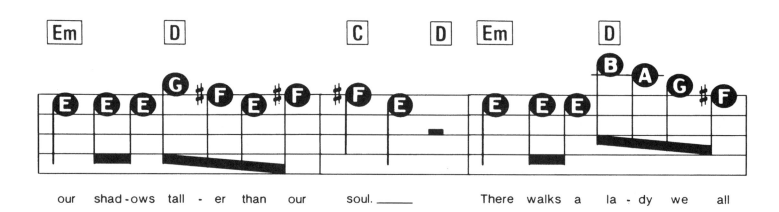

our shad-ows tall-er than our soul. _____ There walks a la-dy we all

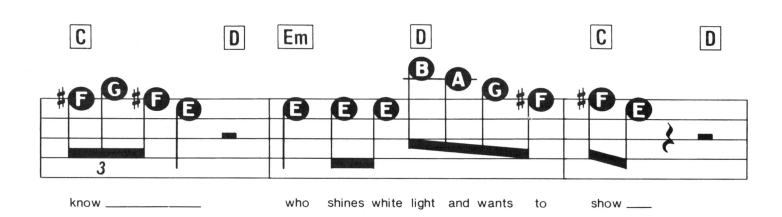

know _____ who shines white light and wants to show ___

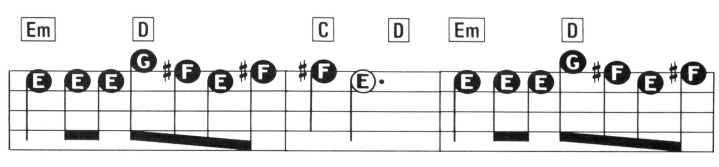

how ev'-ry-thing still turns to gold _____ And if you lis-ten ver-y

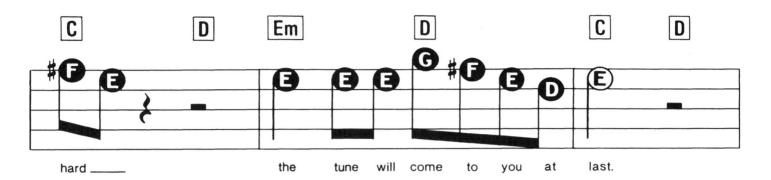

hard _____ the tune will come to you at last.

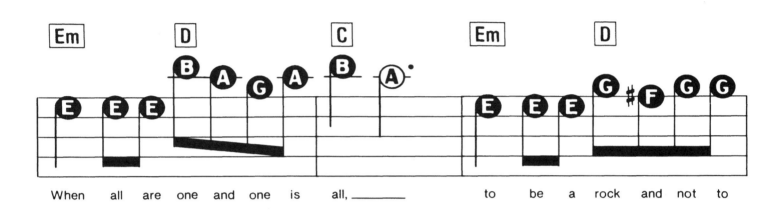

When all are one and one is all, _____ to be a rock and not to

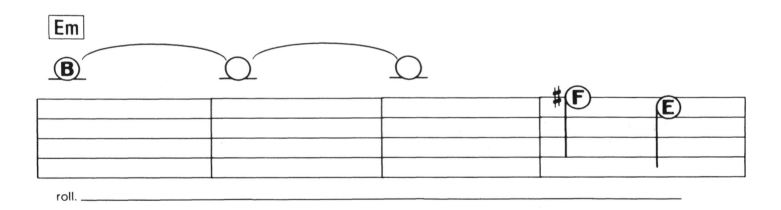

roll. _____

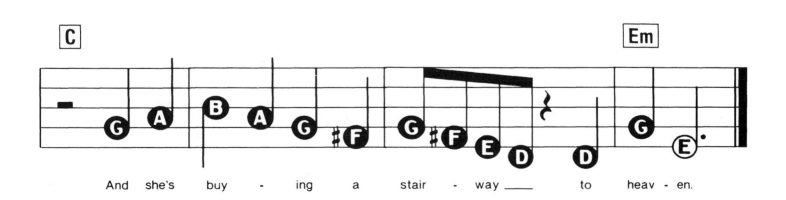

And she's buy - ing a stair - way _____ to heav - en.

Stand By Your Man

Registration 3
Rhythm: Country or Shuffle

Words and Music by Tammy Wynette
and Billy Sherrill

Stand by your man, Give him two arms to cling to,

And some - thing warm to come to when nights are

cold and lone - ly. Stand by your man, And tell the

world you love him. Keep giv - ing all the love you

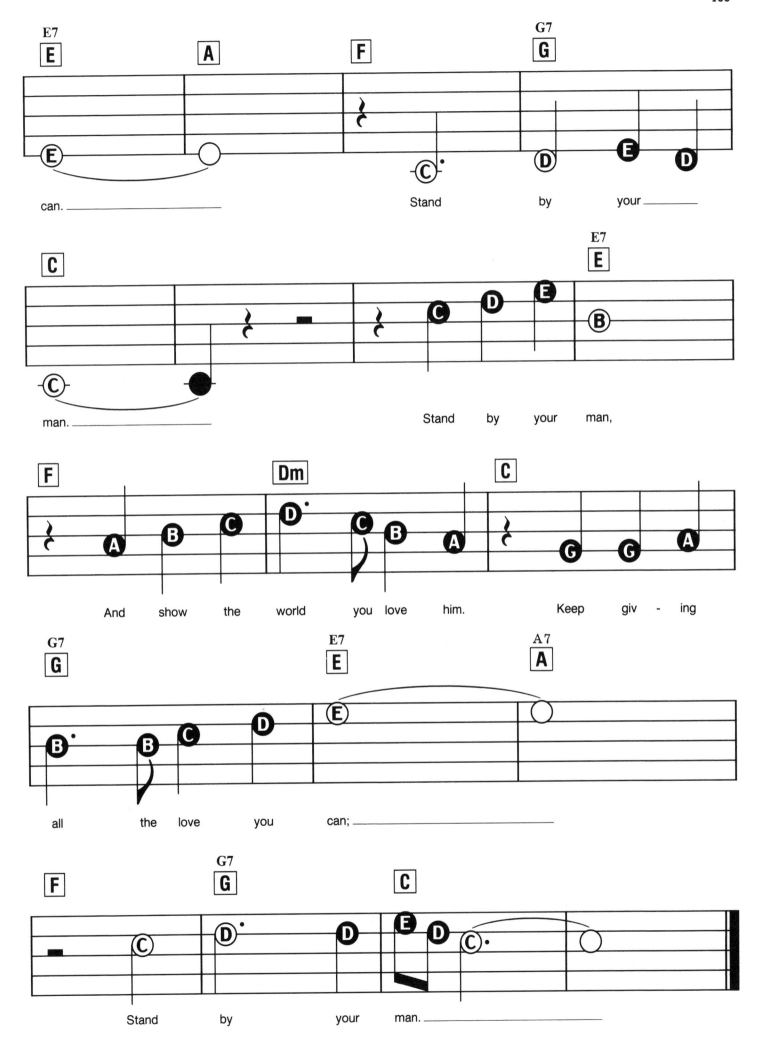

This Land Is Your Land

Registration 9
Rhythm: Country or Swing

Words and Music by
Woody Guthrie

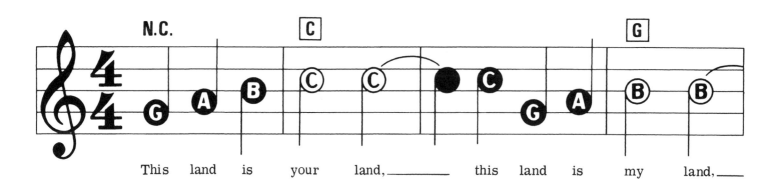

This land is your land, _____ this land is my land, _____

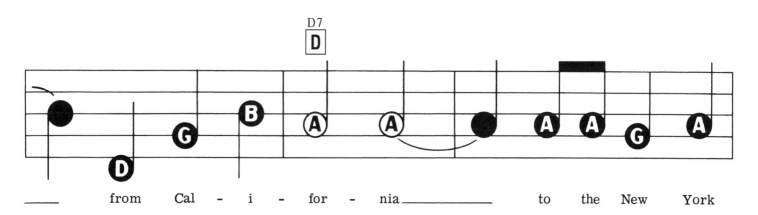

_____ from Cal - i - for - nia _____ to the New York

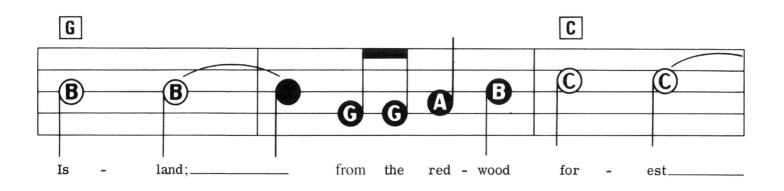

Is - land; _____ from the red - wood for - est _____

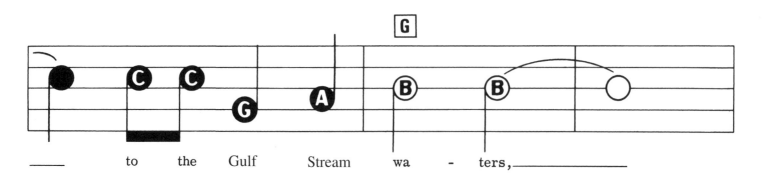

_____ to the Gulf Stream wa - ters, _____

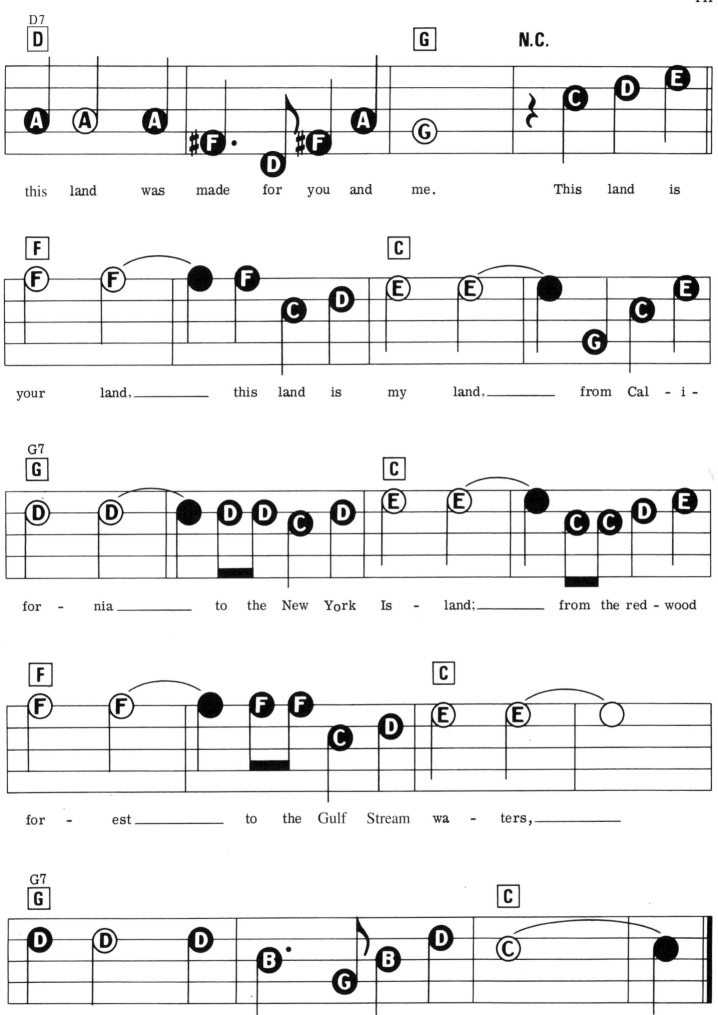

We Are the Champions

Registration 1
Rhythm: Waltz

Words and Music by
Freddie Mercury

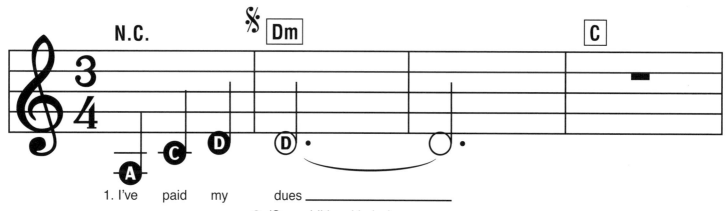

1. I've paid my dues _____

2. (See additional lyrics)

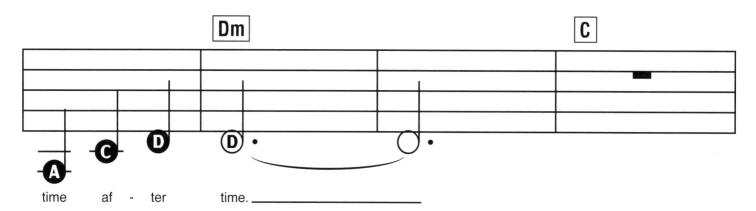

time af - ter time. _____

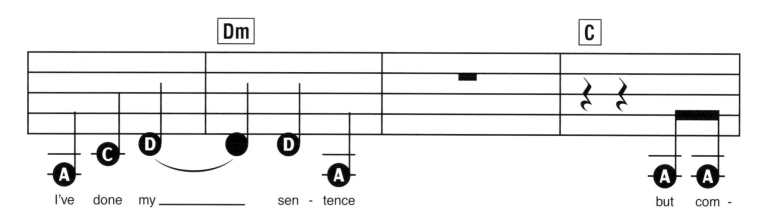

I've done my _____ sen - tence but com -

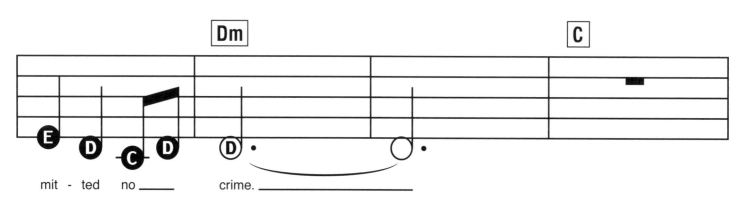

mit - ted no _____ crime. _____

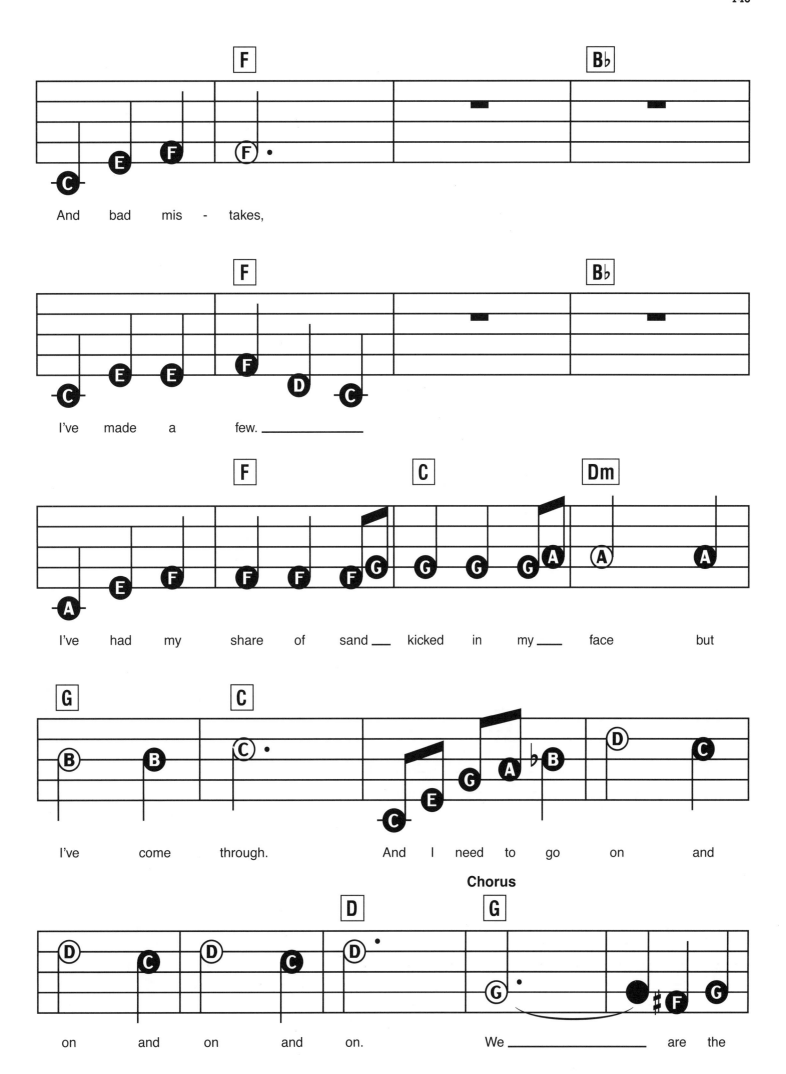

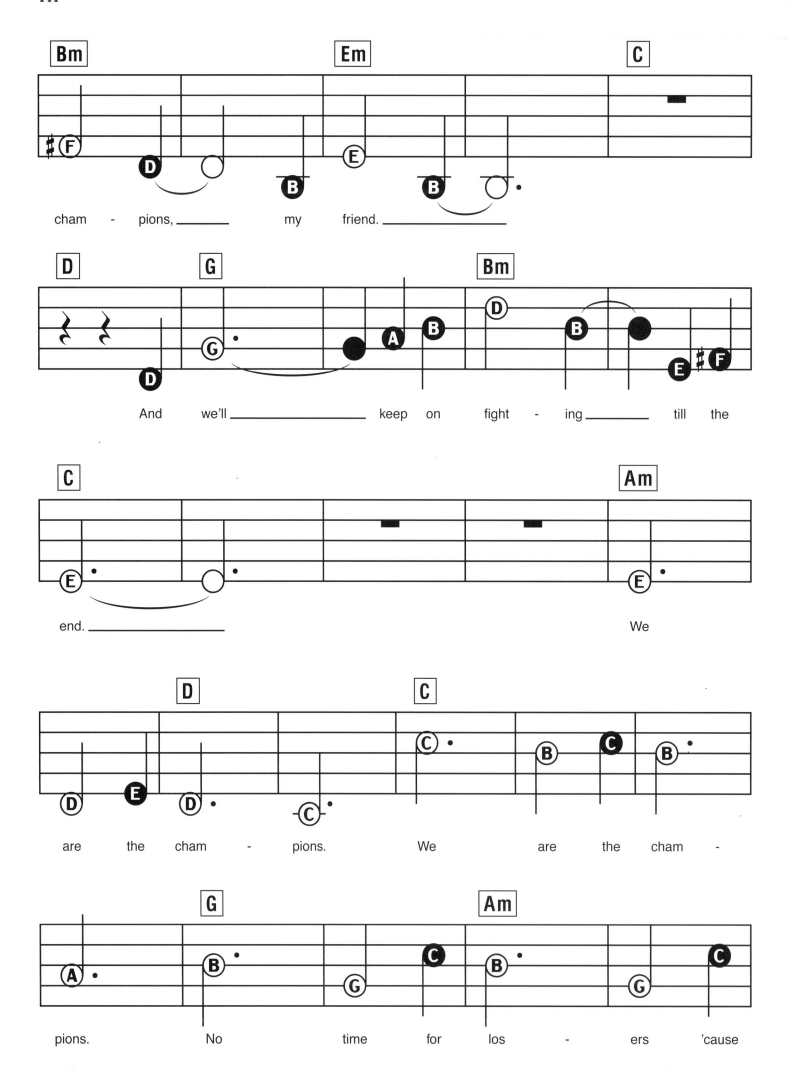

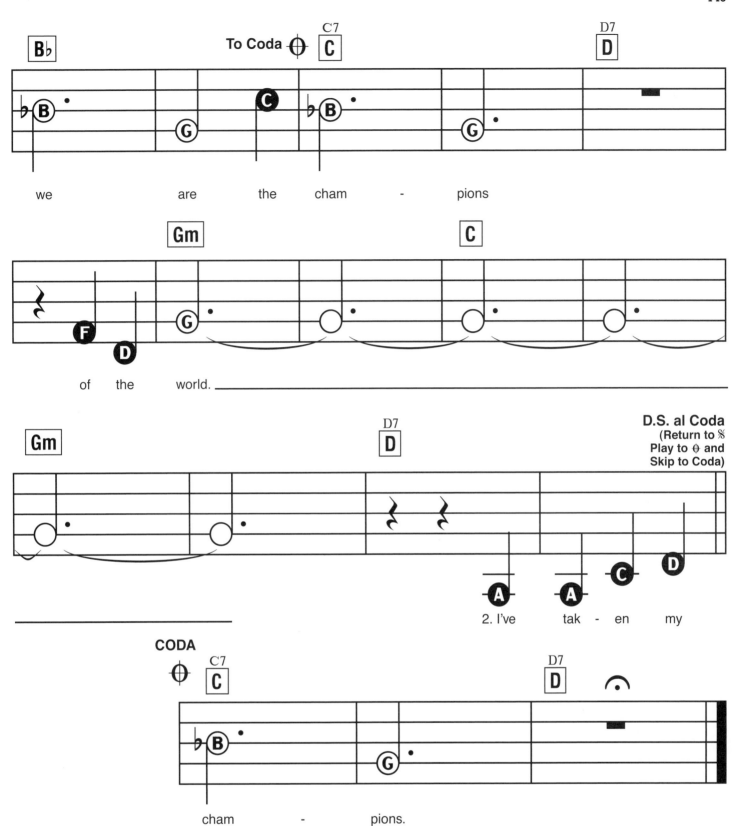

Additional Lyrics

2. I've taken my bows
And my curtain calls.
You brought me fame and fortune
And everything that goes with it.
I thank you all,
But it's been no bed of roses,
No pleasure cruise.
I consider it a challenge before the whole human race
And I ain't gonna lose.
Chorus

Yesterday

Registration 2
Rhythm: Rock or Ballad

Words and Music by John Lennon
and Paul McCartney

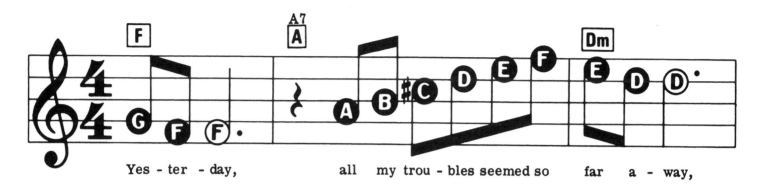

Yes - ter - day, all my trou - bles seemed so far a - way,

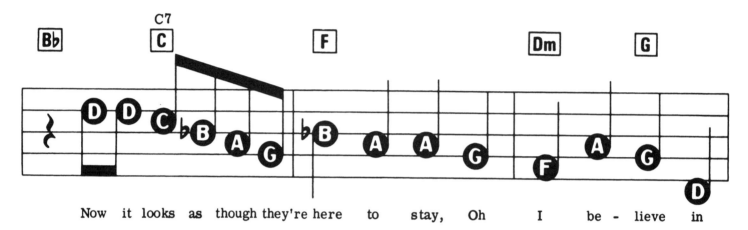

Now it looks as though they're here to stay, Oh I be - lieve in

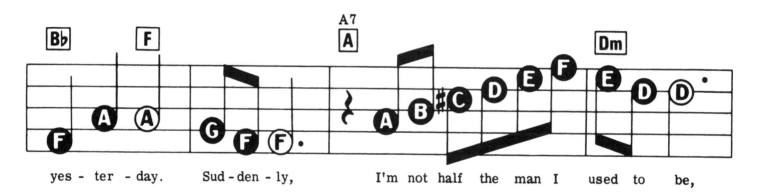

yes - ter - day. Sud - den - ly, I'm not half the man I used to be,

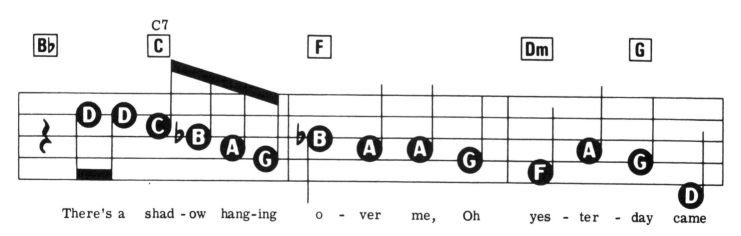

There's a shad - ow hang - ing o - ver me, Oh yes - ter - day came

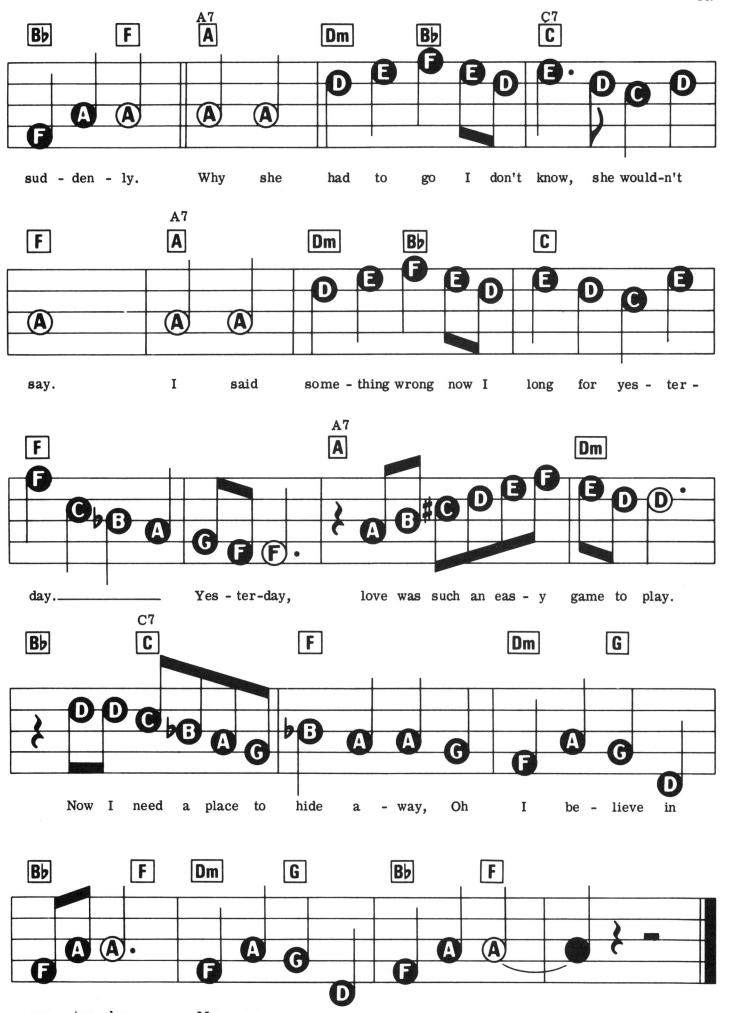

sud - den - ly. Why she had to go I don't know, she would-n't

say. I said some - thing wrong now I long for yes - ter-

day._____ Yes - ter-day, love was such an eas - y game to play.

Now I need a place to hide a - way, Oh I be - lieve in

yes - ter -day. Mm - mm - mm - mm - mm - mm - mm._____

Your Song

Registration 3
Rhythm: Ballad or Pops

Words and Music by Elton John
and Bernie Taupin

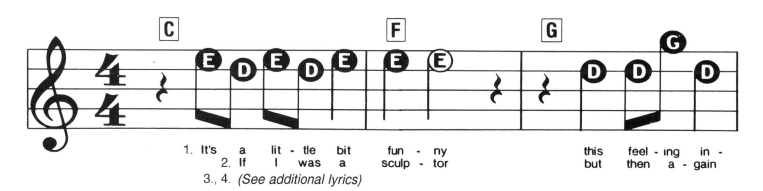

1. It's a lit-tle bit fun-ny   this feel-ing in-
2. If I was a   sculp-tor   but then a-gain
3., 4. *(See additional lyrics)*

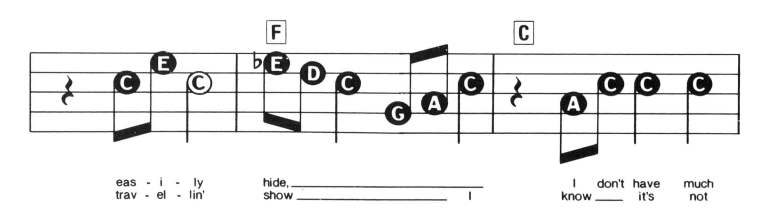

side, _____   I'm not one of those   who can
no, _____ or a   man who _____ makes potions   who in a

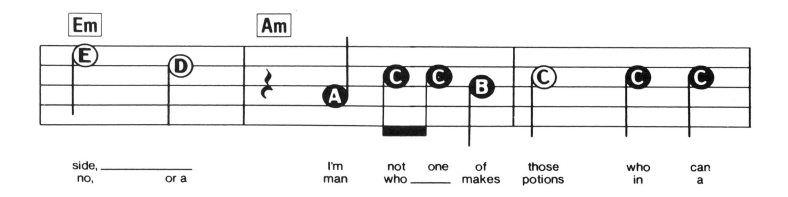

eas - i - ly   hide, _____   I don't have much
trav - el - lin' show _____   I   know ____ it's not

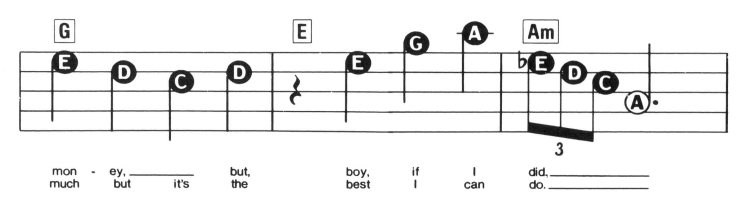

mon - ey, _____ but,   boy, if I   did, _____
much but it's the   best I can   do. _____

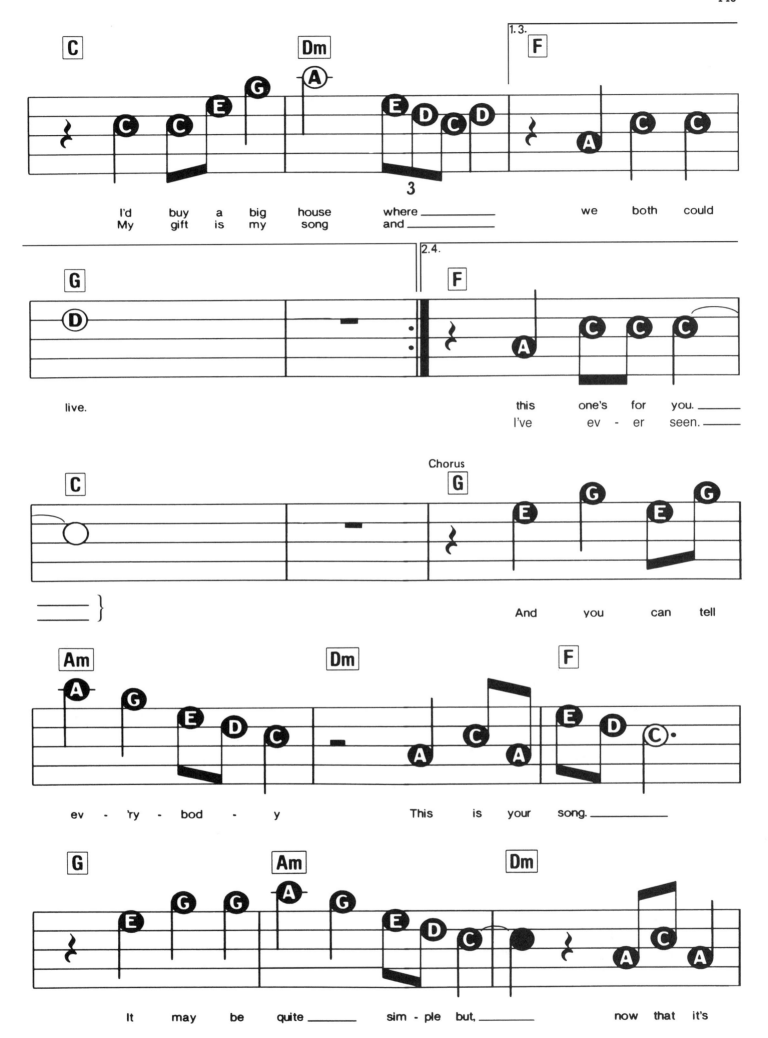

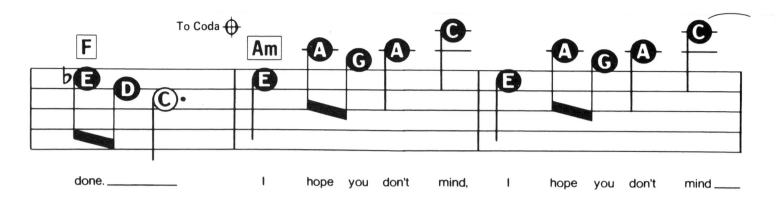

done._____ I hope you don't mind, I hope you don't mind ____

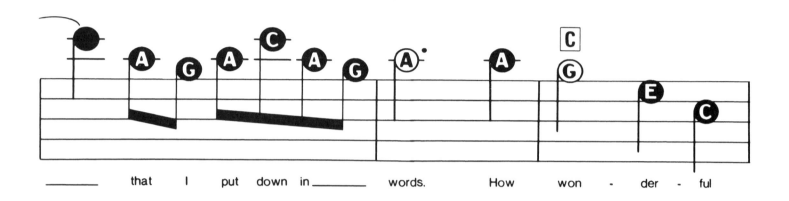

____ that I put down in ____ words. How won - der - ful

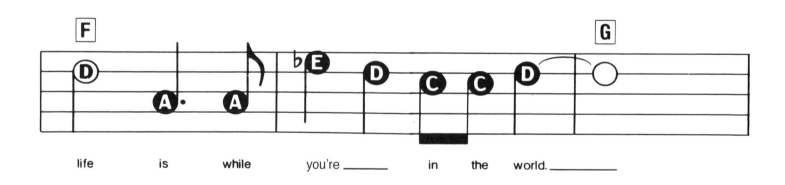

life is while you're ____ in the world. ____

D.C. al Coda
(Return to
beginning,
take 3rd & 4th
endings, Play
till ⊕ and skip
to Coda)

⊕ CODA

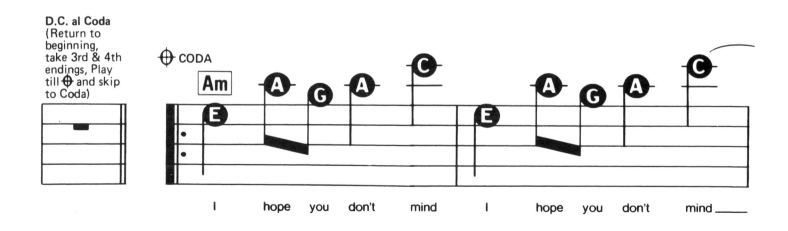

I hope you don't mind I hope you don't mind ____

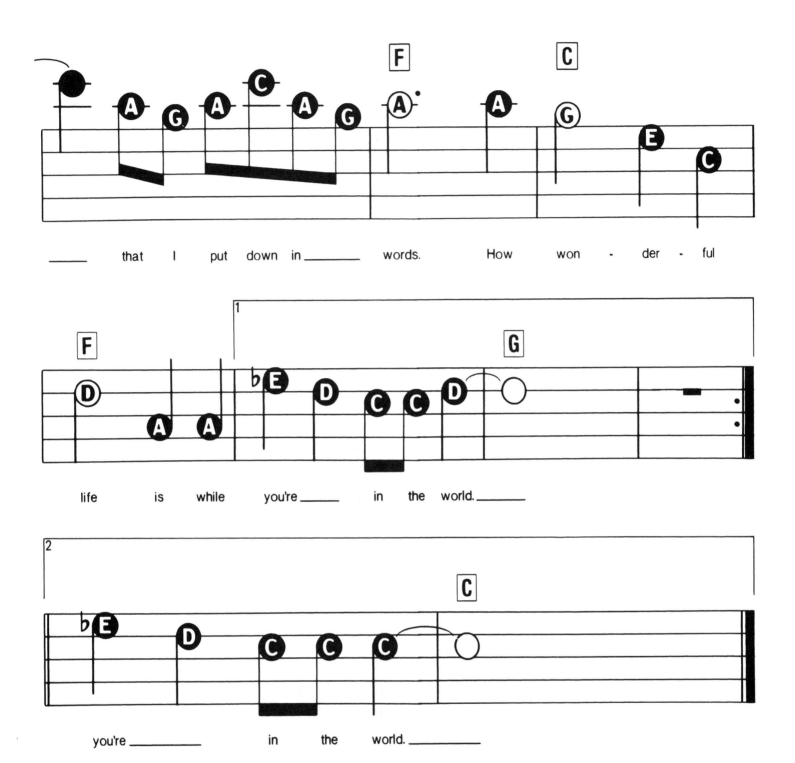

____ that I put down in _____ words. How won - der - ful

life is while you're _____ in the world. _____

you're _____ in the world. _____

Additional Lyrics

3. I sat on the roof and kicked off the moss.
   well a few of the verses, well they've got me quite cross,
   But the sun's been quite kind while I wrote this song,
   It's for people like you that keep it turned on.

4. So excuse me forgetting but these things I do
   You see I've forgotten if they're green or they're blue,
   Anyway the thing is what I really mean
   Yours are the sweetest eyes I've ever seen.
   Chorus

When I'm Sixty-Four

Registration 3
Rhythm: Rock

Words and Music by John Lennon
and Paul McCartney

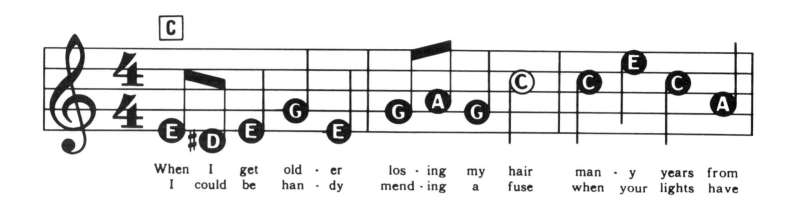

When I get old·er los·ing my hair man·y years from
I could be han·dy mend·ing a fuse when your lights have

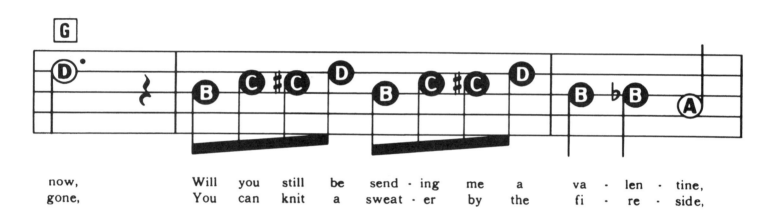

now, Will you still be send·ing me a va·len·tine,
gone, You can knit a sweat·er by the fi·re·side,

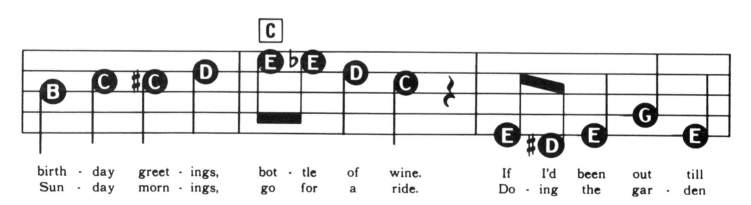

birth·day greet·ings, bot·tle of wine. If I'd been out till
Sun·day morn·ings, go for a ride. Do·ing the gar·den

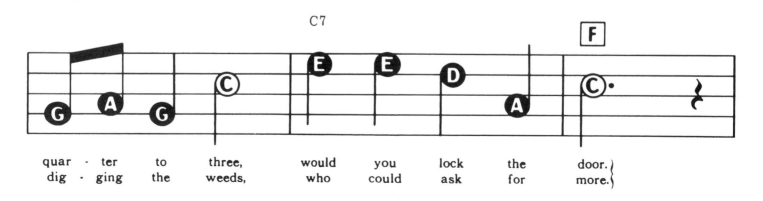

quar·ter to three, would you lock the door.
dig·ging the weeds, who could ask for more.

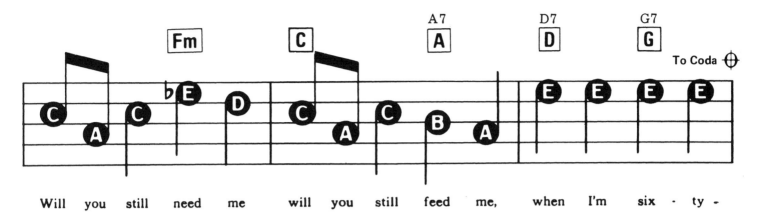

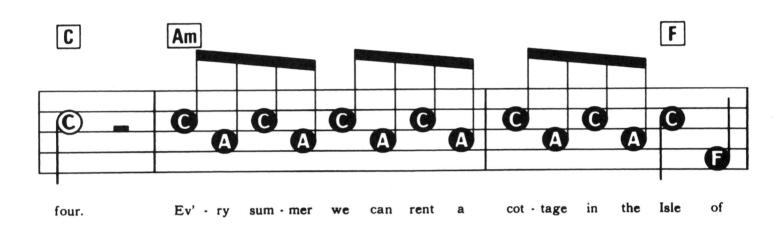

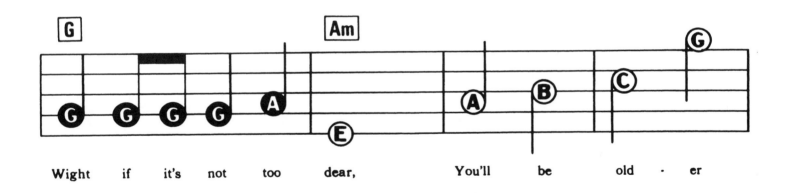

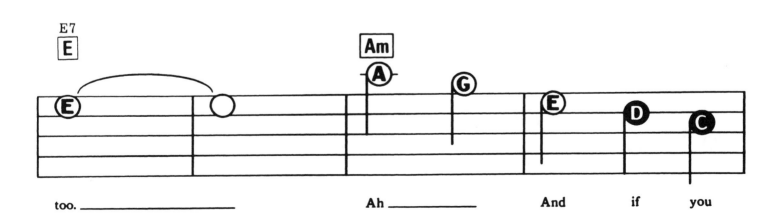

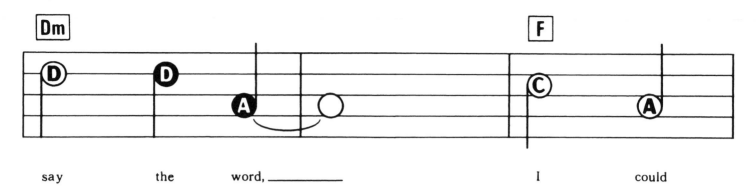

say   the   word, _____   I   could

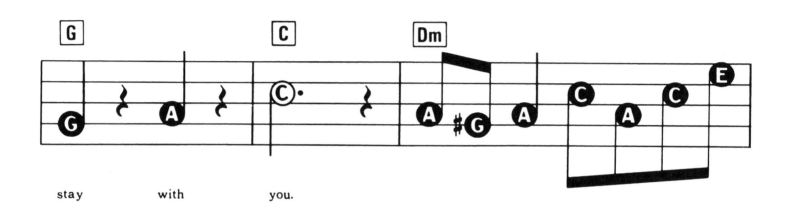

stay   with   you.

D.C. al Coda
(Return to beginning,
Play to ⊕, skip to Coda.)

⊕ CODA

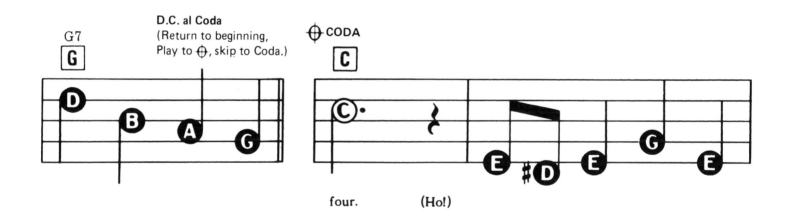

four.   (Ho!)

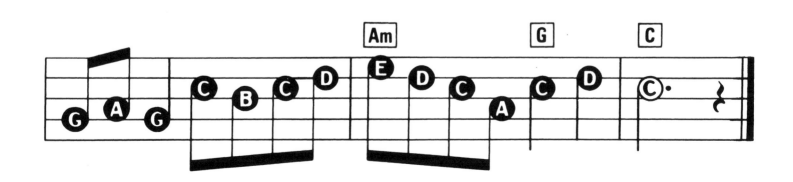

Registration Guide

- Match the Registration number on the song to the corresponding numbered category below. Select and activate an instrumental sound available on your instrument.

- Choose an automatic rhythm appropriate to the mood and style of the song. (Consult your Owner's Guide for proper operation of automatic rhythm features.)

- Adjust the tempo and volume controls to comfortable settings.

Registration

1	Mellow	Flutes, Clarinet, Oboe, Flugel Horn, Trombone, French Horn, Organ Flutes
2	Ensemble	Brass Section, Sax Section, Wind Ensemble, Full Organ, Theater Organ
3	Strings	Violin, Viola, Cello, Fiddle, String Ensemble, Pizzicato, Organ Strings
4	Guitars	Acoustic/Electric Guitars, Banjo, Mandolin, Dulcimer, Ukulele, Hawaiian Guitar
5	Mallets	Vibraphone, Marimba, Xylophone, Steel Drums, Bells, Celesta, Chimes
6	Liturgical	Pipe Organ, Hand Bells, Vocal Ensemble, Choir, Organ Flutes
7	Bright	Saxophones, Trumpet, Mute Trumpet, Synth Leads, Jazz/Gospel Organs
8	Piano	Piano, Electric Piano, Honky Tonk Piano, Harpsichord, Clavi
9	Novelty	Melodic Percussion, Wah Trumpet, Synth, Whistle, Kazoo, Perc. Organ
10	Bellows	Accordion, French Accordion, Mussette, Harmonica, Pump Organ, Bagpipes

FOR ORGANS, PIANOS & ELECTRONIC KEYBOARDS

E-Z PLAY® TODAY PUBLICATIONS

The E-Z Play® Today songbook series is the shortest distance between beginning music and playing fun!
Check out this list of highlights and visit balleonard.com for a complete listing of all volumes and songlists.

HAL•LEONARD®

0421

HAL LEONARD PRESENTS
FAKE BOOKS FOR BEGINNERS!

Entry-level fake books! These books feature larger-than-most fake book notation with simplified harmonies and melodies – and all songs are in the key of C. An introduction addresses basic instruction on playing from a fake book.

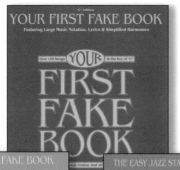

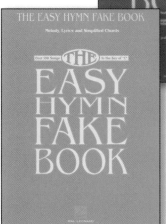
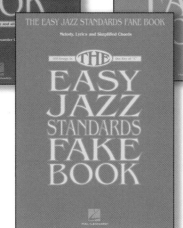
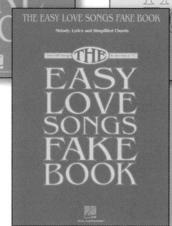
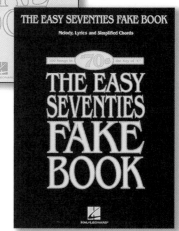

Your First Fake Book
00299529...$22.99

The Easy Fake Book
00240144...$19.99

The Simplified Fake Book
00299494...$22.99

The Beatles Easy Fake Book
00171200 ....$25.00

The Easy Broadway Fake Book
00276670...$19.99

The Easy Children's Fake Book
00240428 ....$19.99

The Easy Christian Fake Book
00240328...$19.99

The Easy Christmas Carols Fake Book
00238187...$19.99

The Easy Christmas Songs Fake Book
00277913...$19.99

The Easy Classic Rock Fake Book
00240389 ....$24.99

The Easy Classical Fake Book
00240262...$19.99

The Easy Country Fake Book
00240319...$22.99

The Easy Disney Fake Book
00275405...$24.99

The Easy Folksong Fake Book
00240360...$22.99

The Easy 4-Chord Fake Book
00118752 ....$19.99

The Easy G Major Fake Book
00142279 ....$19.99

The Easy Gospel Fake Book
00240169 ....$19.99

The Easy Hymn Fake Book
00240207...$19.99

The Easy Jazz Standards Fake Book
00102346...$19.99

The Easy Love Songs Fake Book
00159775 ....$24.99

The Easy Pop/Rock Fake Book
00141667 ....$24.99

The Easy 3-Chord Fake Book
00240388 ....$19.99

The Easy Worship Fake Book
00240265...$22.99

More of the Easy Worship Fake Book
00240362 ....$22.99

The Easy '20s Fake Book
00240336 ....$19.99

The Easy '30s Fake Book
00240335 ....$19.99

The Easy '40s Fake Book
00240252...$19.99

The Easy '50s Fake Book
00240255...$22.99

The Easy '60s Fake Book
00240253...$22.99

The Easy '70s Fake Book
00240256...$22.99

The Easy '80s Fake Book
00240340 ....$24.99

The Easy '90s Fake Book
00240341 ....$19.99

HAL•LEONARD®
halleonard.com

Prices, contents and availability subject to change without notice.

0421
128